How to Make Data Work

Educators are increasingly responsible for using data to improve teaching and learning in their schools. This helpful guide provides leaders with simple steps for facilitating accurate analysis and interpretation of data, while avoiding common errors and pitfalls. *How to Make Data Work* provides clear strategies for getting data into workable shape and creating an environment that supports understanding, analysis, and successful use of data, no matter what data system or educational technology tools are in place in your district. This accessible resource makes data easy to understand and use so that educators can better evaluate and maximize their systems to help their staff, students, and school succeed. With this tried-and-true guidance, you'll be prepared to advocate for tools that adhere to data reporting standards, avoid misinterpretation of data, and improve the data use climate in your school.

Jenny Grant Rankin, Ph.D., teaches at the University of Cambridge for the PostDoc Masterclass and is the former Chief Education and Research Officer at Illuminate Education, an educational technology data systems company. She has been an award-winning teacher, technology coordinator, site administrator, and district administrator.

Other Eye On Education Books
Available from Routledge
(www.routledge.com/eyeoneducation)

Designing Data Reports that Work: A Guide for Creating Data Systems in Schools and Districts
Jenny Grant Rankin

Mentoring is a Verb: Strategies for Improving College and Career Readiness
Russ Olwell

A School Leader's Guide to Implementing the Common Core: Inclusive Practices for All Students
Gloria Campbell-Whatley, Dawson Hancock, and David M. Dunaway

What Connected Educators Do Differently
Todd Whitaker, Jeffrey Zoul, and Jimmy Casas

BRAVO Principal! Building Relationships with Actions that Value Others, 2nd Edition
Sandra Harris

Get Organized! Time Management for School Leaders, 2nd Edition
Frank Buck

The Educator's Guide to Writing a Book: Practical Advice for Teachers and Leaders
Cathie E. West

Data, Data Everywhere: Bringing All the Data Together for Continuous School Improvement, 2nd Edition
Victoria Bernhardt

Leading Learning for Digital Natives: Combining Data and Technology in the Classroom
Rebecca J. Blink

The Trust Factor: Strategies for School Leaders
Julie Peterson Combs, Stacey Edmonson, and Sandra Harris

The Assistant Principal's Guide: New Strategies for New Responsibilities
M. Scott Norton

The Principal as Human Resources Leader: A Guide to Exemplary Practices for Personnel Administration
M. Scott Norton

Formative Assessment Leadership: Identify, Plan, Apply, Assess, Refine
Karen L. Sanzo, Steve Myran, and John Caggiano

Easy and Effective Professional Development: The Power of Peer Observation to Improve Teaching
Catherine Beck, Paul D'Elia, and Michael W. Lamond

Job-Embedded Professional Development: Support, Collaboration, and Learning in Schools
Sally J. Zepeda

Leading Schools in an Era of Declining Resources
J. Howard Johnston and Ronald Williamson

Creating Safe Schools: A Guide for School Leaders, Teachers, and Parents
Franklin P. Schargel

How to Make Data Work

A Guide for Educational Leaders

Jenny Grant Rankin

Routledge
Taylor & Francis Group
NEW YORK AND LONDON

First published 2016
by Routledge
711 Third Avenue, New York, NY 10017

and by Routledge
2 Park Square, Milton Park, Abingdon, Oxon, OX14 4RN

Routledge is an imprint of the Taylor & Francis Group, an informa business

© 2016 Taylor & Francis

The right of Jenny Grant Rankin to be identified as author of this work has been asserted by her in accordance with sections 77 and 78 of the Copyright, Designs and Patents Act 1988.

All rights reserved. No part of this book may be reprinted or reproduced or utilized in any form or by any electronic, mechanical, or other means, now known or hereafter invented, including photocopying and recording, or in any information storage or retrieval system, without permission in writing from the publishers.

Trademark notice: Product or corporate names may be trademarks or registered trademarks, and are used only for identification and explanation without intent to infringe.

Library of Congress Cataloging-in-Publication Data
Names: Rankin, Jenny Grant, author.
Title: How to make data work: a guide for educational leaders/by Jenny Grant Rankin.
Description: New York, NY: Routledge is an imprint of the Taylor & Francis Group, an Informa Business, [2016] | Includes bibliographical references.
Identifiers: LCCN 2015031374| ISBN 9781315665863 (hardback) | ISBN 9781138956155 (pbk).
Subjects: LCSH: Educational evaluation—Data processing. | Educational indicators.
Classification: LCC LB2822.75 .R36 2016 | DDC 371.14/4—dc23
LC record available at http://lccn.loc.gov/2015031374

ISBN: 978-1-138-95614-8 (hbk)
ISBN: 978-1-138-95615-5 (pbk)
ISBN: 978-1-315-66586-3 (ebk)

Typeset in Optima
by Florence Production Ltd, Stoodleigh, Devon, UK

This book is dedicated to
Principal Debra L. Diaz.

*You are the kind of mentor by which educators are most blessed,
and the kind of educator by which students are most blessed.
Thank you for guiding me onto this path so many years ago.*

Contents

Preface　xi
Acknowledgments　xvi
Meet the Author　xviii
eResources　xxi

PART I: INTRODUCTION　1

1. What It Means to Make Data Work　3
   Easy While Still Complex　3
   The Data Analysis Error Epidemic　4
   Do Not Blame Educators　5

2. How to Make Data Work　9
   Data Won't Work without Maximizing All Three Elements　9
   What about Other Stakeholders?　10
   You Can Make Data Work　11

PART II: TOOLS　13

   Be Careful What You Swallow　13
   Evaluate Your Data Tool　16

3. Label　18
   What Is a Label?　18
   Why and How Should Data Be Labeled?　19
   How to Get Labels　26

4. Supplemental Documentation　34
   What Is Supplemental Documentation?　34

Why and How Should Supplemental Documentation
Accompany Data?   35
How to Get Supplemental Documentation   45

5. **Help System**   52
What Is a Help System?   52
Why and How Should a Help System Accompany Data?   53
How to Get a Help System   59

6. **Package/Display**   69
What Is Package/Display?   69
Why and How Should Data Be Packaged/Displayed
Effectively?   70
Examples to Reference If Needed   85
How to Get Effective Package/Display   85

7. **Content**   102
What Is Content?   102
Why and How Should Data Reports Contain Effective
Content?   103
How to Get Effective Content   114

8. **Work With Your DSRP**   122
DSRPs Care about Students and Educators   122
Recognize Your Power Over Change   122
Maintain a Successful Relationship with Your DSRP   124
If You Hit a Wall   132
Conclusion   136

PART III: CLIMATE   139
Other Pieces to Make Data Work   139
What Is Climate?   140
Evaluate Your Data Use Climate   141

9. **Climate Maximization**   144
How to Maximize Climate   144

PART IV: DATA USERS   161
Who Are Data Users?   161
Evaluate Your Data User Support   162

| 10. | Data User Maximization | 164 |

How to Empower Data Users 164

PART V: CONCLUSION   **179**

| 11. | Put It All Together | 181 |

Where to Begin 181
Real-World Implementation 182
Final Words 184

PART VI: APPENDIX   **187**

Appendix: Over-the-Counter Data (OTCD) Standards 189

Preface

Most educators struggle with data use. Three elements need to be maximized in order to improve educators' understanding and use of data: the data use climate, the data users themselves (such as through professional development), and the data tools employed to view and analyze data. No matter how perfect a job educator leaders do in maximizing one of these three areas, staff will continue to struggle with data use until all three elements are properly handled. This book shares research-based strategies for improving educators' data use by maximizing all three elements: climate, data users, and data tools.

Audience, Book Structure, and Content

This book is for educator leaders (e.g., data coaches, principals, grade level or department chairs, district administrators, etc.) who share education data with others and/or support educators' data use. Different book parts will help you with each of the three elements that control the success of data use.

This Book Is for You—Yes, *You*—No Matter Your Role

Nearly every school district in the USA utilizes a data system (Gartner & Bill and Melinda Gates Foundation, 2014), and many other countries have similar widespread use. The rare school districts that do not have data systems are either extremely small and remote (e.g., 30 students in the entire district) or encountered a temporary mishap (e.g., their data system provider folded).

Tools

The next part—"Tools"—will help you identify and overcome shortcomings in the data system, reports, and/or tools you and your staff use to work with data. This section begins with:

- **Evaluation** tools (e.g., online surveys and evaluation forms) you can use to assess and better understand your particular data system and/or data reports.

Each subsequent chapter will provide the following for a specific component that can enhance your data reporting environment:

- **Description** of the component and how to spot it in your reporting environment;
- **Summary** of why the component should be implemented within your school district's own reporting environment (e.g., research indicating even just one component improves educators' data analysis accuracy by up to 436 percent), as well as some details on how the component should function.

> Standards shared in this book have been shown to improve educators' data analyses by up to 436 percent.

- **How to get** the component; sometimes this involves a third party (such as a vendor) controlling your data system, in which case emails have already been written for you to copy/paste and send, lessons and templates have already been made to assist this party with implementation, etc.

In short, this section will make it easy for you to get more out of your data reporting environment, regardless of its source, so it *actively* improves data use, saves educators' time, and reduces educators' frustration.

Climate

Your data tools' transformation will also complement other efforts to improve data use so you are not working harder than you need, to acquire poorer results than you, your staff, and your students deserve. Yet even well-presented data can be misused if the environment within which staff uses data is not constructive.

This book's "Climate" section will help you maximize climate through straightforward steps. The book section will delineate:

- **What** constitutes a data use climate, and climate's role in data use;
- **Evaluation** tools you can use to assess and better understand your particular data use climate;
- **How to maximize** your particular climate to facilitate optimum data use.

Data Users

Of course, we can't forget the educators who are using the data with the tools you perfect and within the climate you maximize. Educators' preparation for data use—as well as their support throughout this task—is fundamental.

This book's "Data Users" section will help you empower data users through straightforward improvements to professional development (PD), staff-based supports, and more. The book section will delineate:

- **Who** is considered a data user and what role the data user plays in data use;
- **Evaluation** tools you can use to assess and better understand how your particular staff is being supported;

Preface

- **How to train and support** your particular site's data users to facilitate optimum data use.

A number of resources are available for download as eResources at www.routledge.com/9781138956155.

Conclusion and Resources

The book will end with a chapter on integrating the three elements that control the success of data use, as well as resources to help. When you use this book to tackle educators' tools, climate, and support, you "make data work" for educators who view and use data.

> ### *Every Educator Has a Data System*
>
> Your data system is:
> - the place you visit on your computer/device to view your data (school data, student data, etc.);
> - where your printed data reports (that someone else might give you) are coming from.
>
> You can have multiple data systems.

Furthermore, every school district's teachers and administrators use data reports. At this point, data use is a required part of adhering to the professional standards of our time. So, your staff is using data from some sort of data system/report provider (DSRP).

When it comes to benefitting—so your colleagues can benefit—from this book, it does not matter who you are. You do not even have to have an official leadership role to step forward so staff is better supported in using data. For example:

- **Tools**—You do not have to be a district administrator or the person overseeing your district's data system to play a vital role in advocating for your data system's or data reports' improvement.

- **Climate**—You do not have to be a principal or the lead person composing the district's vision to play a vital role in facilitating a better data use climate.
- **Data Users**—You do not have to be a district administrator or the person overseeing funds and professional development to play a vital role in getting colleagues the kind of PD and support they need to best use data.

You might officially be a leader of educators (all of whom should read this book), but any educator can use this book to improve staff's data use environment, and thus improve staff's data use.

If data is to be made easy for staff to understand and use, your voice is needed. *Your* voice. Every educator—and especially every educator leader—has an important perspective on staff's data needs and a role in seeing those needs are met.

Whoever you are, you are in prime position to advocate for the data system, data use climate, and data PD your colleagues need. Embrace this role so staff and students can benefit. Do not wait for someone else to do it, because every advocate is needed for fast and effective improvement.

Reference

Gartner & Bill and Melinda Gates Foundation. (2014). *Closing the gap: Turning SIS/LMS data into action: Report: Education community attitudes toward SIS/LMS solutions.* Retrieved from www.turningdataintoaction.org/sites/default/files/reports/education_community_attitudes_toward_sis_lms_solutions.pdf

Acknowledgments

The research that went into this book was accompanied by a career learning the topic's intricacies and putting data use into practice. I thus owe deep gratitude to the educators who oversaw this experience, and the staff at the sites where it took place. These include Buena Park Junior High School under Debra Diaz's leadership; Orangeview Junior High School under Dr. Kevin Astor's leadership; Saddleback Valley Unified School District under Dr. Kathy Dick's leadership (with additional accolades going to Margaret Stewart, my unparalleled secretary at the time and a data whiz in her own right, as well as the supportive JL4 team); and Illuminate Education under Lane Rankin's leadership. Each of these individuals is a prime example of how strong data leadership benefits staff and—especially—students. I am also very grateful to the educators who lent their wisdom to the book in the form of chapter vignettes. These include Kris Boneman, Carol Bright, Dr. Sharon Cordes, Debra Diaz, Dr. Margie Johnson, George Knights, and Mike Morrison. The experiences they shared are only a snapshot of the wealth of expertise they offer our profession. I thank Ann Barreto, as well, for being so kind as to review the book in its early stages and offer helpful feedback. I am grateful to the incomparable educators who reviewed the book and offered their endorsements. These include Debra Diaz, Gustavo Reyes, Jennifer Kagy, Julie Duddridge, Dr. Margie Johnson, and Rufus Thompson. I owe additional thanks to Rufus Thompson, along with Dr. Gail Thompson, for their mentorship and continual encouragement. Whenever my steam threatened to wane, these bosses inspired me to persist, and I am continually inspired by them. I also owe additional thanks to Dr. Margie Johnson for her support with whatever I needed from the beginning—when this book was just forming—and through to the end. Her early involvement in implementing OTCD

Standards is testament to the kind of educator she is: aware of what is needed even before the rest of the field catches up. I also thank my daughter, Piper Rankin, for her understanding whenever Mommy was on her laptop again. Her five years of life have all seen me stealing time for this book, and I look forward to celebrating its completion with her. Equally understanding was my husband, Lane Rankin, who I thank for believing in the project's importance and supporting me with love. I am so blessed to have such a wonderful partner in life. I also appreciate that Lane (CEO/Founder of Illuminate Education, which provides data-related edtech) granted use of screenshots from his help system. Greg DeVore (CEO and Co-Founder of Blue Mango Learning Systems) kindly provided details used when describing the ScreenSteps-created help system, and will be highlighted in more detail in my next book. I thank my sons—Clyde Rankin, Zach Rankin, and Tyler Rankin (who lend their genius to the data edtech field)—and friends for always being so positive when I spoke of my research and this book. The same goes for my mother, Nancy Grant, who is my unwavering rock of encouragement and love (and the "Gammy time" with Piper sure helped the book's progress). I also thank Michael Walker for kindly providing my author photo (a great photographer who gets it on the first try). In addition, I owe special thanks to Heather Jarrow, my amazing editor at Routledge/Taylor & Francis Group. Enthusiastic from the start, Heather was the key to this dream of mine coming true. There are things in this book not covered in most books on the same topic, yet Heather was not scared off from this lack of convention. Rather, she saw the need for it, provided sage advice, and helped the book become a tool for change. I also thank Karen Adler, an editorial assistant at Routledge/Taylor & Francis Group, for answering my many questions in such a welcoming way. I feel so blessed to have been helped by the caring souls acknowledged here.

Meet the Author

Award-winning educator Dr. Jenny Grant Rankin, who teaches at the University of Cambridge for the PostDoc Masterclass, has a Ph.D. in education featuring a specialization in school improvement leadership. She is an active member of Mensa and many educational organizations, particularly within the areas of data, assessment, and technology.

After working in higher education overseeing a university's Visual Arts and Information Technology Departments, Dr. Rankin pursued a rewarding career in K-12 public education. She served as a teacher (of junior high school English, Newspaper, and AVID), teacher on special assignment (TOSA) and technology coordinator, junior high school assistant principal, district administrator (overseeing assessment and data use for a 35,000-

Meet the Author

student school district) and chief education and research officer (CERO) for Illuminate Education (an educational technology data systems company where she was able to impact data use at hundreds of school districts across the USA).

Dr. Rankin's books relate to data, education, and technology. Her papers and articles on this book's topic have appeared in such publications as ASCD's *Educational Leadership, CCNews: Newsletter of the California Council on Teacher Education* (CCTE), *EdCircuit, Ed-Fi Alliance Blog, EdSurge* (funded by *the Washington Post*), *EdTech Review, Edtech Women, Edukwest, eSchoolNews, International Society for Technology in Education* (ISTE) *EdTechHub,* and *OnCUE: Journal of Computer Using Educators* (CUE). Dr. Rankin's work has also appeared in the *Mensa Bulletin* and conference proceedings.

Dr. Rankin has given a TED Talk on this topic at TEDxTUM and presents this research annually at the U.S. Department of Education's Institute of Education Sciences (IES) National Center for Education Statistics (NCES) STATS-DC Conferences and at the International Society for Technology in Education (ISTE®) Conference. She also presented on this topic at the American Educational Research Association (AERA); California Council on Teacher Education (CCTE) Conference; California Educational Research Association (CERA) Conferences; Carnegie Foundation Summit on Improvement in Education; Classroom 2.0's Learning 2.0 Conference; Connect: Canada's National Learning and Technology Conference; K-12 Online Conference; Learning Revolution Conference; Leadership Innovation Event at Montfort College, Chang Mai, Thailand; OZeLIVE! Australia: Ed Tech Down Under Conference; Society for Information Technology and Teacher Education (SITE) Conferences; Technology Information Center for Administrative Leadership (TICAL) School Leadership Summit; University of California, Irvine (UCI) Digital Learning Lab; University of California, Los Angeles (UCLA) and National Center for Research on Evaluation, Standards, and Student Testing (CRESST) Conference; and others.

Winning Teacher of the Year was a favorite honor, as was having the U.S. flag flown over the United States Capitol at the request of the Honorable Christopher Cox, U.S. Representative, in recognition of Dr. Rankin's dedication to her students. Her more recent awards include the #EduWin Award, EdTech's 2014 Must-Read Higher Education Technology Blogs List, finalist for EdTech Digest's Trendsetter Award, SIGNL Award for Twitter Followers Momentum, and Association for the Advancement of

Computing in Education (AACE) Academic Expert. Her research website is also included on MIT's concise List of EdTech Blogs and Sites.

Dr. Rankin has served as judge for the University of Pennsylvania Graduate School of Education's prestigious Milken-Penn Graduate School of Education Business Plan Competitions and the California Student Media Festivals (CSMF) sponsored by PBS SoCAL, Computer Using Educators (CUE), and Discovery Education. Dr. Rankin was also paid to examine alignment issues related to the Common Core State Standards (CCSS) summative assessments as part of the Smarter Balanced Assessment Consortium (SBAC) Alignment Study, and she also served on the Smarter Balanced Assessment Consortium (SBAC) Panel for Achievement Level Setting.

In addition, Dr. Rankin has served on research committees for the International Society for Technology in Education (ISTE), the Society for Information Technology and Teacher Education (SITE), and the California Council on Teacher Education (CCTE). She also served on the Panel of Experts and the Advisory Board for the New Media Consortium (NMC) Horizon Report: 2015 K12 Edition, honored with a special listing and acknowledgment in the report. Dr. Rankin also served as reviewer for the *Handbook of Research on Innovations in Information Retrieval, Analysis, and Management* from IGI Global and is an expert reviewer (reviewing for the journal *Educational Researcher* and multiple awards) for the American Educational Research Association (AERA). She regularly shares new research on this book's topic at www.overthecounterdata.com and https://twitter.com/OTCData (Twitter handle @OTCData).

eResources

Keep an eye out for the eResources icon throughout this book, which indicates a resource is available online. Many of the tools in this book can be downloaded, printed, used to copy/paste text, and/or manipulated to suit your individualized use. You can access these downloads by visiting the book product page on our website:

www.routledge.com/9781138956155

Then click on the tab that reads "eResources" and then select the file(s) you need. The file(s) will download directly to your computer.

Tools

- OTCD Standards
- Details on Evidence (supporting every one of the OTCD Standards)
- Needs Matrix (there are both pdf and xlsx versions)
- Data Use Reference Tool (in Word format to facilitate modification)
- Sample Data Types to Support Data Analyses
- Sample Questions Data Can Help Answer
- Reference Sheet Templates (there are both doc and docx versions)
- Reference Guide Templates (there are both doc and docx versions)

eResources

- Sample Reference Sheets
- Sample Reference Guides
- Report Before and After Examples
- Evaluations in Online Survey Format
- Evaluations in Word Format
- Email Verbiage to Copy/Paste
- School District's Opportunities to Influence DSRP (diagram)

Also available online:

- Glossary

PART I

Introduction

Everything should be as simple as it can be,
but not simpler.

—Albert Einstein
(said to Louis Zukofsky)

What It Means to Make Data Work

Easy While Still Complex

If you look at a pile of a thousand puzzle pieces, you will not easily know what picture the puzzle can illustrate. If you pretend the complex puzzle is simple and try to draw conclusions from only a few pieces, you risk misunderstanding. Only when the pieces are properly assembled is the image clear and your understanding of it accurate.

If puzzle pieces were presented to you in assembled form from the beginning, you would save time, avoid misunderstanding, and instantly see the final picture. The puzzle would still be complex, but it would be presented in a format one would deem easy to understand.

Education data is complex.[1] Thousands of data elements are collected in an education data system for reporting purposes (Colorado Department of Education, 2008). But, like a puzzle, something inherently complex *can* work for you if you honor its complexity and use the best way to present its various pieces.

If you share education data with others and/or support educators' data use, the way you present and share data is vital. All your efforts to improve data use will be unnecessarily stunted, and you will be working too hard, if you do not take simple steps to spur improvement in the way your data is presented. Essentially, you and your staff would be trying to understand a puzzle that has not been properly assembled. Instead, you can make your data easy to understand and use.

Yet even well-presented data can be misused. An effective data use climate and the right support for staff are essential to making data work. When you tackle educators' tools, climate, and support, you will cover the workable data issue from all angles. For you and staff, making data work means:

Introduction

- **easier data use**
- **improved data use** (accurate data analyses, appropriate data use, better data-informed decision-making, etc.)
- **saved time**
- **reduced frustration**.

You can make data truly work for you and your staff instead of against you. If you maximize your tools, climate, and staff support, you can unlock the data's potential to help all stakeholders and students.

The Data Analysis Error Epidemic

The National Center for Education Statistics estimates less than 2 percent of school districts in the USA are able to turn data into information educators can use (Sparks, 2014). Even when educators do use data, they often misunderstand it. For example, national studies of districts known for strong data use found teachers showed difficulty with question posing, data comprehension, and data interpretation, and teachers answered only 48 percent of questions correctly when drawing inferences from given data (U.S. Department of Education Office of Planning, Evaluation and Policy Development [USDEOPEPD], 2009, 2011). An abundance of research

View/Analyze Reports	Make Decisions	Impact Students
• 44% of educators use data systems directly, but the majority view printed versions of reports others generate for them (Underwood, Zapata-Rivera, & VanWinkle, 2008). • At most, 48% of educators' data interpretations are accurate (USDEOPEPD, 2009, 2011).	• Educators then make decisions informed by their understanding of the data. • If educators are not making appropriate data analyses, they are not likely making appropriate decisions influenced by those flawed analyses.	• Educators' data-informed decisions impact students (as the main reason they are being made is *to* impact students). • Decisions based on flawed data analyses are likely to negatively impact students.

Figure 1.1

upholds these findings: educators use data to inform decisions, but they commonly use it incorrectly. Figure 1.1 is a synopsis of how educators' data-informed decision-making works.

Do Not Blame Educators

Sure, everyone has room to improve, but educators constitute good candidates for data use in that they are generally:

- **highly skilled**—e.g., 95 percent of teachers are considered "highly qualified" by No Child Left Behind (NCLB) standards (American Institutes for Research, 2013);
- **well-educated**—e.g., 99 percent of American teachers have bachelor's degrees, 48 percent have master's degrees, and over 7 percent have more advanced graduate degrees (Papay, Harvard Graduate School of Education, 2007);
- **intelligent**—e.g., educators have above-average IQs;[2]
- **care about students**—e.g., 85 percent of teachers say they became teachers because they wanted to make a difference in children's lives (Bill and Melinda Gates Foundation, 2014), and 90 percent of students believe their teachers care about their learning (Northwest Evaluation Association, 2014);
- **embracing data use**—e.g., most educators are eager to analyze and then act on the data they see (Hattie, 2010; van der Meij, 2008);
- **embracing technology use**—e.g., teachers indicated overwhelming support for using technology to improve learning, and 85 percent of teachers reported daily use of technology to support teaching (Bill and Melinda Gates Foundation, 2012);
- **employing approaches within their power** to grow professionally—e.g., districts devote 1 percent to 8 percent of their operating budgets to providing professional learning (Killion & Hirsh, 2012); the quality of training and supports can always be improved, but at least some is taking place.

Introduction

Thus the sharing of statistics on data analysis failures should not be mistaken as a criticism of the highly qualified and proactive educators who are making analysis mistakes. Rather, if a more-ideal-than-average client base continues to make so many analysis errors when viewing data, it is important to consider and remedy problems with the reporting tools, climate, and support they are provided.

Even when a vendor or other third party supplies the data system/reports, educator leaders can easily influence these tools. As the next section covers, trying to improve data use *without* improving data reporting is like trying to support someone in guessing what a puzzle illustrates without assembling the pieces. If poor data use climate and poor staff support are also at play, making sense of the data puzzle becomes even less likely.

Notes

1. The *Wall Street Journal* (Izzo, 2012) reflects this book's use of "data *is*" and "data *are*," see blogs.wsj.com/economics/2012/07/05/is-data-is-or-is-data-aint-a-plural/.

2. The average IQ of a college graduate is 121+ and of most Ph.D. recipients is 132+ (Hurley, 2012), whereas the average IQ of the general population is considered 100 (Weiss, 2009); since only 30.4 percent of the general population of an age comparable to teachers holds a college degree (Pérez-Peña, 2012), whereas nearly all educators are college graduates (at a minimum), educators' IQs are likely to be above those of the general population as a whole.

References

American Institutes for Research (AIR). (2013). *Most teachers "highly qualified" under NCLB standards, but teacher qualifications lag in many high poverty and high minority schools.* Retrieved from www.air.org/reports-products/index.cfm?fa=viewContent&content

Bill and Melinda Gates Foundation. (2012). *Innovation in education: Technology and effective teaching in the U.S.* Retrieved from www.edsurge.s3.amazonaws.com/public/BMGF_Innovation_In_Education.pdf

Bill and Melinda Gates Foundation. (2014). *Primary sources: America's teachers on teaching in an era of change: A project of Scholastic and the Bill and Melinda Gates Foundation* (3rd ed.). Retrieved from www.scholastic.com/primarysources/download-the-full-report.htm

Colorado Department of Education. (2008). *Statewide Longitudinal Data Systems (SLDS) grant: Progress overview, July 2008*. Retrieved from www.cde.state.co.us/sites/default/files/documents/slds/download/pdf/slds_progressoverview_as_of_july_2008.pdf

Hattie, J. (2010). Visibly learning from reports: The validity of score reports. *Online Educational Research Journal*. Retrieved from www.oerj.org/View?action=viewPaper&paper=6

Hurley, D. (2012, April 22). Can you build a (better brain?) *New York Times*, MM38.

Izzo, P. (2012, July 5). Is data is, or is data ain't, a plural? *Wall Street Journal*. Retrieved from blogs.wsj.com/economics/2012/07/05/is-data-is-or-is-data-aint-a-plural/

Killion, J., & Hirsh, S. (2012, February). The bottom line on excellence: A guide to investing in professional learning that increases educator performance and student results. *JSD: The Learning Forward Journal, 33*(1). Oxford, OH: Learning Forward.

Northwest Evaluation Association (NWEA). (2014). *Make assessment matter: Students and educators want tests that support learning*. Portland, OR: Author.

Papay, J., Harvard Graduate School of Education. (2007). *Aspen Institute datasheet: The teaching workforce*. Washington, DC: The Aspen Institute.

Pérez-Peña, R. (2012, February 24). Milestone is passed as 30 percent of U.S. adults report having a college degree. *New York Times*, A17. New York, NY: New York Times Company Inc.

Sparks, S. D. (2014, July 25). Can states make student data useful for schools? *Education Week*. Retrieved from blogs.edweek.org/edweek/inside-school-research/2014/07/can_states_turn_slag_data_into.html

Underwood, J. S., Zapata-Rivera, D., & VanWinkle, W. (2008) Growing pains: Teachers using and learning to use IDMS®. *ETS Research Memorandum. RM-08–07*. Princeton, NJ: ETS.

U.S. Department of Education Office of Planning, Evaluation and Policy Development. (2009). *Implementing data-informed decision making in schools: Teacher access, supports and use.* United States Department of Education (ERIC Document Reproduction Service No. ED504191).

U.S. Department of Education Office of Planning, Evaluation and Policy Development. (2011). *Teachers' ability to use data to inform instruction: Challenges and supports.* United States Department of Education (ERIC Document Reproduction Service No. ED516494).

Van der Meij, H. (2008). Designing for user cognition and affect in a manual. Should there be special support for the latter? *Learning & Instruction, 18*(1), 18–29.

Weiss, V. (2009). National IQ means transformed from Programme for International Student Assessment (PISA) scores, and their underlying gene frequencies. *Journal of Social, Political and Economic Studies.* Munich, Germany: German Central Office for Genealogy.

How to Make Data Work

Data Won't Work without Maximizing *All* Three Elements

There are three key elements that can be maximized to make data use easy and accurate: climate, data users, and data tools. This book will help you with all three, particularly an element far too often overlooked in efforts to improve data use: tools used for data analyses. Many educators do not ask for more than a data system that gives all educators access to data, when there is so much more their data systems could do to actively help educators make easy, good use of data. For example, one change shared in this book has been shown to *quadruple* educators' understanding of given data. Educator leaders can advocate for such changes in their data tools, and this book makes the process simple.

Yet in education, turning to tools for support with data analysis is less common than turning to leaders or professional development (PD) (Marsh, Pane, and Hamilton, 2006). PD and staffing-based supports (strong leadership, data coaches, professional learning communities (PLCs), collaboration, etc.) hold great potential to improve educators' data use, and most districts are already utilizing them on some level. However, many findings indicate PD and staff supports are not omnipotent, meaning while they are recommended they will not bring a 100 percent accuracy rate to educators' data analyses. For example:

- In a study where teachers received PD in educational measurement/assessment, all teachers struggled afterwards with statistical terms and measurement concepts (Zapata-Rivera & VanWinkle, 2010).

Introduction

- Knowledge management research indicated knowledge is hard to share with others, even when the intention to share it is there, especially when power or status is involved (Cho & Wayman, 2009).

Given extensive evidence of their benefits, PD and staffing-based supports should definitely be employed as resources allow. This book will help educator leaders provide PD, other staff supports, and a data use climate that help make data easy to use.

However, with educators making so many data analysis errors even in districts known for strong data PD, staff, and culture, traditional data analysis interventions are clearly not enough. We add *to* these supports' impact when we improve how data is presented within our data tools.

We provide educators with the most effective data use environment when we take specific steps to target all three elements that impact data use. Tools, data users, and climate can work together to make data easy for staff to understand and use.

> We provide educators with the most effective data use environment when we . . . target tools, data users, and climate in ways that make data easy for staff to understand and use.

What about Other Stakeholders?

Educators are not the only stakeholders who use education data. Students, parents, non-educators involved in education processes, reporters, politicians, non-profit staff, policy advocates, reporters/media, product providers, service providers . . . many types of people need to understand the education data they view.

This book focuses on educator data users, but that does not mean other stakeholders like students should not be supported in data use, as indeed they should. Many of the concepts covered in this book will also lead to improved data use for other stakeholders, yet other resources can help you provide those stakeholders with added assistance specific to their roles.

You *Can* Make Data Work

With whatever reporting tools educators opt to use, there are three key stages when educators can influence the data they and their colleagues analyze. All three of these stages play important roles in data use, as do the stages that come after data is reported (e.g., implementation of data-informed decisions). However, only one of these three stages provides a chance to put data into a "workable" format, and thus this is the only stage this book concerns, see Figure 2.1 below.

Education data is inherently complex. Pretending it is simple is as foolish as only looking at one of a puzzle's many pieces to conclude the puzzle's meaning. Treating education data as if it is simple, results in the use of poor reporting, which directly contributes to flawed data analyses. But, like a puzzle, complex data *can* be made easy if you honor its complexity and present its varied pieces in the most effective way.

Producing Data	Adding/Housing Data	Reporting/Viewing
• Education data comes from a variety of sources and concerns a variety of stakeholders and institutional aspects.	• Many practices are vital to having clean, comprehensive, accurate, usable data in your data system or report suite.	• The stage where data is reported to educators is where we have the chance to make data work so it is easy to understand, analyze, use correctly, etc.
• Although this book references a matrix of sample data types and sources (see "Sample Data Types to Support Data Analyses" at www.tandf.net/books/details/9781138956155/), this book is not devoted to this data stage.	• Resources such as Data Quality Campaign's 10 Essential Elements (www.dataquality campaign.org) and Ed-Fi Alliance's interoperability standards (www.ed-fi-org) can help you maintain quality data.	• Improved data tools, complemented by effective climate and support for data users, allow us to actually make data usable, even though data's nature remains complex.
• E.g., this book does not concern writing quality assessment questions, how to survey stakeholders, creating effective rubrics, etc.	• This book is not mainly devoted to this data stage; rather, it concerns what to do with the quality data.	• This book concerns this data reporting/viewing stage and related standards to make data work.

Figure 2.1

The improved data tools, user skills, and climate you acquire with the help of this book will actively improve educators' data use, save educators' time, and reduce educators' frustration. You *can* make data work for those who view and use it.

References

Cho, V., & Wayman, J. C. (2009, April). Knowledge management and educational data use. Paper presented at the 2009 Annual Meeting of the American Educational Research Association, San Diego, CA.

Marsh, J. A., Pane, J. F., & Hamilton, L. S. (2006). *Making sense of data-driven decision making in education: Evidence from recent RAND research.* Santa Monica, CA: RAND Corporation.

Zapata-Rivera, D., & VanWinkle, W. (2010). A research-based approach to designing and evaluating score reports for teachers. *ETS Research Memorandum. RM-10–01.* Princeton, NJ: ETS.

PART

II

Tools

> Minimize the extent to which [educators] need to actively analyze data . . . We give such tools to physicians and military decision makers; education is no less complex and no less important.
>
> —U.S. Department of Education Office of Educational Technology, 2012, p. 49

Be Careful What You Swallow

If something is "over-the-counter" it is easy to access and use successfully. On this note, it would be negligent and dangerous for over-the-counter medicine to be sold without a label other than a mere heading like "Cold" or "Flu." Rather, an over-the-counter product offers embedded guidance (e.g., a detailed label and more) explaining the product's purpose, ingredients, dosage instructions, dangers, and anything else you would need to know in order to use the contents correctly.

Tools

Educators use data to "treat" students, given data's proven benefits as an added resource for understanding students' needs. Most educators acquire this data from reports, generally generated within a data system or created by a colleague using exported data. Most teachers even use data while on their own (USDEOPEPD, 2009).

Unfortunately, the data reporting tools educators use to consume data typically do not provide supports (or enough supports) to help educators understand how to use the reports' contents properly (VanWinkle, Vezzu, & Zapata-Rivera, 2011). Educators are using data that is not presented in an "over-the-counter" format, so there are no embedded supports to ensure the data is used easily and *correctly*. The ramifications are rampant errors with most data analyses (covered in Chapter 1).

Rather than leaving people to guess (often incorrectly) how to properly use and understand a potent tool like medicine or data, a tool that is over-the-counter offers components to actively reduce detriments and increase benefits. Consider the impact of not providing usage guidance directly on a life-affecting tool:

- If medicine offered no embedded usage guidance, users would not know how to properly use the contents. Lives could be hurt. Thus this never happens; over-the-counter products always actively support people in using the product's contents.
- If education data systems/reports offer no embedded usage guidance, users do not know how to properly use the contents. Lives can be hurt. Yet this commonly happens. Conversely, over-the-counter data actively supports people in using the data.

Continuing with the pharmaceutical example helps illustrate each component's importance when it comes to how data is communicated to educators, see Table 3.1.

When these five components are added successfully to a data reporting environment, educators can easily know what the data means and how to use it. The good news is that educator leaders can often acquire these components with little effort on their own part.

Table 3.1

Over-the-Counter Component	You Have Seen It Look Like This in Over-the-Counter Medicine	It Can Look Like This in Data Reporting Tools
Label	The container label provides the name and information answering questions like, "How many should I take?" and "What are the possible side effects?", etc.	The report has a clear and concise title, and an annotation like a footer provides the information most relevant and important to using the report's data properly.
Supplemental Documentation	Not all the information a user needs to know can fit on the label, so a folded-up piece of paper is enclosed within the package to offer further explanation.	Similarly, explanatory information specific to each report, like a reference sheet and reference guide, can accompany each report via links and handouts.
Help System	Users want an online help system; e.g., 50 million people use WebMD every year (Kronstadt, Moiduddin, & Sellheim, 2009).	An online help system can offer comprehensive lessons on using the data system *and* on data analysis.
Package/ Display	How the product is displayed and packaged helps communicate its correct purpose and use.	How data is organized and displayed, such as layout that encourages *correct* analyses for each particular report, helps to avoid confusion.
Content	The ingredients of the product are vital; they have to be effective, user-appropriate, and not expired.	The contents of each report and the report suite as a whole should be effective, audience-appropriate and not expired.

Evaluate Your Data Tool

You might want to evaluate your data system/reports before following the upcoming chapters' recommendations to advocate for these tools' improvement. If so, online resources can assist your evaluation, and you can choose the format(s) you prefer:

> ### Time-Saving Resource
>
> Use the Educational Leader's Evaluation of Data System/Report Tool in whichever format you prefer (online survey vs. Word document).

- **Online tool evaluation** (in survey format): you can complete to receive results (and an evaluation score) automatically emailed to you.

- **Word file of tool evaluation** (which you can edit as necessary to suit your site): you can complete on your computer or in printed form to evaluate your data system/reports while also adding notes concerning steps you plan to take to improve areas (which the next five chapters will help you determine).

The evaluation will make more sense once you have read this book. Refer to this book as necessary (particularly the next five chapters) to better understand any of the evaluation's questions.

Use the evaluation in whatever way is most helpful for you. For example, you and your colleagues might discuss and complete the evaluation as a district department, or you might reflect on all of the evaluation's questions by yourself and write notes beside each question.

Determining what constitutes a "yes" or a "no" answer on the evaluation should be based on what you (or the group with which you are working) deem to be desirable yet reasonable for your site's current use of the data tool. Determine what level of adherence constitutes a "Yes" answer versus a "No" answer before beginning the evaluation. For example:

- If you choose 80 percent as your threshold, you would determine a "Yes" answer to the question "Does each report have its own, distinct title" if 80 percent or more of the available reports have their own, distinct titles.

You can return to this survey as often as you like to reevaluate your data tools over time.

References

Kronstadt, J., Moiduddin, A., & Sellheim, W. (2009, March). *Consumer use of computerized applications to address health and health care needs: Prepared for U.S. Department of Health and Human Services, Office of the Secretary, Assistant Secretary for Planning and Evaluation.* Bethesda, MD: NORC at the University of Chicago.

U.S. Department of Education Office of Educational Technology. (2012). *Enhancing teaching and learning through educational data mining and learning analytics: An issue brief.* Washington, DC: Author.

U.S. Department of Education Office of Planning, Evaluation and Policy Development. (2009). *Implementing data-informed decision making in schools: Teacher access, supports and use.* United States Department of Education (ERIC Document Reproduction Service No. ED504191).

VanWinkle, W., Vezzu, M., & Zapata-Rivera, D. (2011). Question-based reports for policymakers. *ETS Research Memorandum. RM-11–16.* Princeton, NJ: ETS.

Label

What Is a Label?

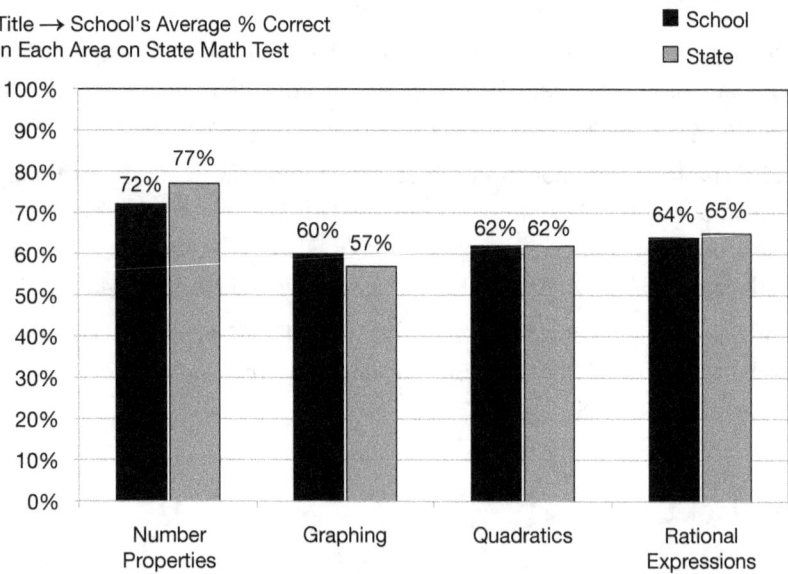

Figure 3.1

Would you use over-the-counter medicine from a bottle that read "Flu" and nothing else: no more in the title to let you know if it is for a cold flu versus stomach flu, and no label outlining how many pills to take, symptoms treated, ingredients, or dangers to consider? Of course you would not. Taking medicine from an unmarked or marginally marked container would be negligent and dangerous. Yet educators use data system reports featuring data with nothing other than poor titles (e.g., test title), and they use these reports to make decisions that impact kids. Such practice results in slow, hard, and flawed data use.

Data that is "over-the-counter" is reported with two types of labels:

- an effective report title (sometimes called a header), which is the text at the top of the report; and
- an effective footer (or other annotation), which is text located directly on the data report (e.g., the bottom of the page if printed, and the bottom of the screen or image if viewed on a computer screen).

The purpose of the title and footer is to help the user easily understand and use the data.

Please see Figure 3.1.

Why and How Should Data Be Labeled?

The need for thorough report labels is better understood when education data's complex nature is better understood.

- **Example:** Consider Figure 3.2, which is a typical format seen in data system reports. The left bar of each pairing on the graph represents a single school and charts the average percent of questions its students answered correctly within four areas known as content clusters.

While this test is for one particular state's math proficiency test, the reporting style is common for other assessments, as well. Most people would assume educators could easily understand such a report and use the data it contains to make decisions. So, take a look at the graph and answer this question:

Tools

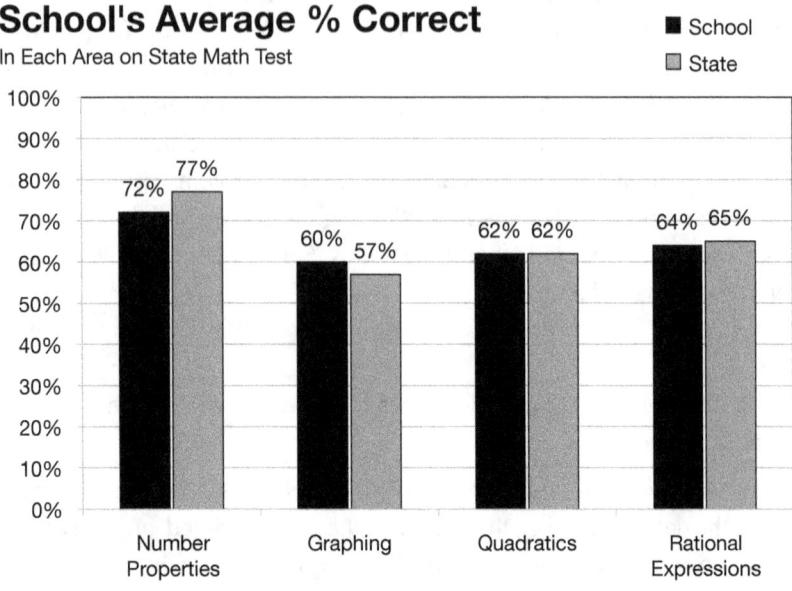

Figure 3.2

- Which area (e.g., *Number Properties, Graphing,* etc.) is most likely to be the school's weakness?

This is not a trick question concerning multiple measures, as you *can* determine what is—according to this report—most likely to be the school's weakness. It is safe to assume you know the importance of using multiple measures and thus you would use this report to determine a possible weakness, which you could then consider along with other measures, as well.

So, what's your answer to the above question? Considering this report, most educators would identify *Graphing* as a possible school weakness because it has the school's lowest percent correct. However, *Graphing* was actually the cluster in which the school performed *best.*

> The scores' true implications are the exact opposite of what educators commonly assume.

As it happens, content clusters on this particular test differ in difficulty, much like your classes differed in difficulty when you were in high school (e.g., a parent might be more pleased with your "B" in Honors Physics than with your "B" in Introduction to Physical Education: the same grade but different implications). Thus the school's highest percent correct for a cluster does not necessarily indicate its strength, and its lowest percent is not necessarily its weakness.

The state that designed this test recommends comparing the School % to the State % (i.e., the degree to which the school beat the scores of minimally proficient students state-wide), since state performance provides us with a picture of which areas were harder for students and which were easier. In other words, you could use this formula:

- School % − State % = #

The cluster with the highest difference (highest # using the above formula) could be a school strength, and the cluster with the lowest difference (lowest # using the above formula) could be a school weakness. Using this formula, *Number Properties* was the cluster in which school lagged the most behind state.

Given this added information, most educators have a completely new sense of what the data means. If they had proceeded without this information and assumed the data was simple enough to understand without it, 89 percent of educators' conclusions would have been wrong (Rankin, 2013) . . . and those faulty conclusions would have shaped actions that would impact students. Even multiple measures offer little help if their implications are misunderstood, as well. Labels such as titles and footers offer the chance to embed important analysis guidance *directly within* data reports where it is hard for educators to overlook them.

Titles

When viewing reports, teachers indicate the desire for clearer titles (Hattie, 2010). This need extends to educators in non-teaching roles, as well. All reports should be clearly titled and labeled so all stakeholders (i.e., educators and non-educators) can easily understand the data (James-Ward, Fisher, Frey, & Lapp, 2013).

Assuming relevant data has already been collected and inputted into the data system, the initial step in most educators' data investigations is to search for particular reports in the data system or report suite that are best suited for the question, theory, or topic under investigation. This involves searching and skimming report titles. Sadly, common problems with data report titles include:

- not facilitating recommended data investigation practices (e.g., they are test-driven rather than topic-driven);
- poorly communicated report content and nature;
- unnecessary inconsistency;
- too many words;
- words do not maximize information communicated about the report.

Consider the last two problems listed above. Too much text can overwhelm users and increase the chances of the words being ignored entirely (Hattie, 2010; Zapata-Rivera & VanWinkle, 2010). It would be ill-advised to try to accommodate all of a report's descriptors in its title, but there are many instances in which a title can provide users with a better understanding of the report contents before even opening the report. The trick for titles is being as concise as good sense allows while also communicating as much as possible of the *most pertinent* information a user needs to know when determining if this is the report he or she needs.

- **Example:** Why say "Multi-Yr" in the title of a report that allows up to 3 years of data to be displayed when "3-Yr" is shorter and more descriptive? Using half as many characters, "3-Yr" adds less clutter to the title while simultaneously communicating more.

> **Too Wordy and Vague:**
> *Multi-Yr Subgroup Report*
>
> **Concise and Clear:**
> *3-Yr Subgroup Comparison*

Even if a district has only added two years of data to the system generating this report (and thus only two years of data are displayed), users would know not to waste time searching for a different report if they wanted three years of data, as this was the right report. They would simply contact a system administrator to request that an additional year's data be added.

Footers

If *all* educators had time to read *all* the technical reports, post-test guides, and research reports for *all* of their datasets (many of these ranging from 150–600 pages), they might not need annotations like footers or other textual support on their data reports. If you consider how busy educators are, you will understand educators do not have time to read and memorize everything that will help them analyze each dataset. For example, half of teachers and principals alike report they are regularly under great stress (Metropolitan Life Insurance Company, 2013).

Footers written by education data experts can alert users to possible missteps and help them avoid analysis errors most common for the particular data being viewed. Consider the graph example provided earlier in this chapter. Now, imagine the potential of a footer at the bottom of that particular report stating:

- Content clusters vary in difficulty, so a school's highest % correct does not necessarily indicate its strength, or the lowest % its weakness. Reference how well School performed in relation to State, which is graphed in purple.

. . . and possibly providing an example:

- e.g., School's score of 60% minus State's score of 57% = +3 (School did well in *Graphing*), whereas School's score of 72% minus SMP's score of 77% = –5 (School did more poorly in *Number Properties*).

The concept explained in this footer can be difficult to grasp, but imagine how much *more* complicated it would be if the report did not contain this textual guidance at all. Likewise, the design of this sample report (the way in which results are graphed) is highly flawed and not carrying its weight

Tools

in assisting good analysis (something covered later in the "Package/Display" chapter). However, it is the most common way in which this particular data is graphed.

Many data systems (one of which you might be using) market within multiple states, and while they change labels and which reports they choose to display for users, they often do not devote the necessary time to customizing the report format to best suit educators' analyses. The data report example just provided, though not ideal, is nonetheless very typical. While this is a problem that should ideally be remedied (also addressed in "Package/Display"), imagine how much more important the easy inclusion and customization of footers becomes when a report's format is misleading.

A quantitative study (Rankin, 2013) presented 211 educators (of varied backgrounds and roles at nine elementary and secondary schools) with graphical and tabular reports, which these educators then used to answer multiple data analysis questions. Each data report set looked the same and contained the same data from assessments participants likely worked with regularly, yet the report sets differed in terms of whether or not they offered added textual guidance to help users analyze the reports' contents. Significant findings:

- Educators whose data reports featured footers (which offered analysis guidance specific to those reports) used the footers 73 percent of the time.

> Footers increase data analysis accuracy by 307–336 percent.

- In terms of relative and absolute differences, educators' data analyses were 307 percent more accurate (with a 23 percentage point difference) when a footer was present and 336 percent more accurate (with a 26 percentage point difference) when respondents specifically indicated having used the footers.

The footers used in the Rankin (2013) study followed OTCD Standards covered in this book. Thus, if your data system provider implements the standards with fidelity, you can expect results similar to a 307–336 percent increase in educator colleagues' data analysis accuracy when using those reports.

Over-the-Counter Data Standards

An ideal data reporting environment should reflect the OTCD *Label* Standards, which stipulate research-based ways data systems/reports can provide titles and footers. These standards can be found in the back of this book if you want to learn more about what qualifies as effective titles and footers.

Good News

You are likely not the one who has to implement these standards. You only need to know they exist so you can ask for them. If you do want advanced support creating your own labels, read *Designing Data Reports that Work: A Guide for Creating Data Systems in Schools and Districts*.

However, you are likely not the one who has to implement these standards. This book you are reading is for educator leaders, but there is a second book out there written for data system/report providers. Those who design, program, manage, and provide the data system/reports you use (as well as educators who design or build some of their own data reports) can read *Designing Data Reports that Work: A Guide for Creating Data Systems in Schools and Districts* by Dr. Jenny Grant Rankin for help with the process of implementing every OTCD *Label* Standard.

Experience from the Field

"The footers are the first things I look at when I open data reports. When I look at data, I have to look at those footers because their information tells me what data I'm actually looking at. This lets me know how to interpret it correctly so I can use it correctly. If a data

> report doesn't have a footer offering guidance, it's all just numbers—not information.
>
> The significance of this can be seen in how data is orally presented. For example, in so many presentations (like we often see administrators do), the presenters just throw numbers at you. The data doesn't have any meaning in this format. Conversely, our assistant superintendent, Dr. Ramon Miramontes, put up some information and actually said, 'Now these are just numbers; let's break this down and talk about what these numbers really mean.' Then he basically shared what a data report's footer—if it had a footer—would share. That was one of the first times I saw data in a presentation used in a correct and meaningful way.
>
> With footers on our data system's reports, we get this kind of information all the time. There's so much power in our data system, with the different reports that can be used to look at data. There's a world of information in there, but teachers feel overwhelmed just thinking about it. If teachers aren't afraid to access the data reports – which is something report footers can help with – think of how that information could help us help our students."
>
> —Carol Bright, History Teacher and Former Department Coach
> Buena Park Junior High School

How to Get Labels

You are likely not the one who has to implement effective titles and footers for your data reports, which requires having the capacity to manipulate those reports. If you do not have this ability (e.g., if a third party, such as a vendor, provides your data system/reports), the fastest and easiest way for you to get effective titles and footers is to advocate for them.

If Someone Other Than You Provides Your Data System/Reports

The Best Approach: DSRPs are largely driven by client request. The best way for you to get effective report titles and footers is to ask for them.

Time-Saving Resource

Copy/paste text from the following page's email into your own email.

This book makes it easy for you to request effective labels by providing an already-written email (shown on an upcoming page) you can send to your data system/report provider (DSRP). Simply copy/paste text from the electronic copy into an email, and modify/personalize your message as needed.

Before you send the email:

1. Determine whether effective labels are, indeed, missing from your data reports. Referencing the *Label* standards in the back of this book can help you make this determination. Then you can enhance your email with details about specific problems you have noted.
2. Determine who at the DSRP is the best contact (this could be the Customer Service Department, but there is likely an implementation manager or other team member through whom you will find faster results).
3. Determine whether your district requires enhancement requests to go through a particular district administrator. In most cases it is appropriate for you to send the email yourself, but even then it is an advantage if district administrators *also* contact the DSRP advocating for effective titles and footers.
4. It is also recommended you read this book in its entirety so you can prioritize requests you send to your DSRP.

Tools

See the "Work with Your DSRP" chapter for details on how this initial step can initiate change in your data system/reports. That chapter will also guide you if any follow-up is necessary.

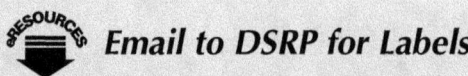
Email to DSRP for Labels

Dear Data System/Report Provider,

I noticed our district's data reports do not adhere to the Over-the-Counter Data *Label* Standards that stipulate research-based ways to provide effective titles and footers on education data reports. Adherence to these *Label* standards is necessary to best support educators' easy use and thorough understanding of reports' data. Consider:

- Only 48 percent of teachers' inferences based on given data are accurate at districts with strong data cultures (U.S. Department of Education Office of Planning, Evaluation and Policy Development, 2009), with other educators' analyses being poorer.

- A footer (adhering to the Over-the-Counter Data *Label* Standards) more than *triples* educators' data analysis accuracy (307 percent increase) when it is present on a data report, and data analysis accuracy increases by 336 percent when educators specifically indicate having used the footer (Rankin, 2013).

- When present, effective footers are used by educators 52 percent of the time (Rankin, 2013).

Please attune our data system/reports to adhere to the research-based Over-the-Counter Data *Label* Standards. These resources can help you:

- Over-the-Counter Data Standards are available with other eResources (including details on the research behind each standard) at wwww.routledge.com/9781138956155 (the *Label* standards are on pages 1–2).

- Read the book *Designing Data Reports that Work: A Guide for Creating Data Systems in Schools and Districts*, by Dr. Jenny Grant Rankin. This guide explains how to implement each reporting standard within a data system/reports (offering specific examples, illustrations, etc.).

Thank you very much for your time and assistance. Adhering to these standards will offer tremendous help to educators and students.

—Me

Rankin, J. G. (2013). *Over-the-counter data's impact on educators' data analysis accuracy*. ProQuest Dissertations and Theses, 3575082. Retrieved from http://pqdtopen.proquest.com/doc/1459258514.html?FMT=ABS

U.S. Department of Education Office of Planning, Evaluation and Policy Development (2009). *Implementing data-informed decision making in schools: Teacher access, supports and use*. United States Department of Education (ERIC Document Reproduction Service No. ED504191)

The Less Desirable Approach: Ideally your DSRP will comply with the email you sent in the previous ("The Best Approach") section so you and your staff can benefit from effective labels. This book's "Work With Your DSRP" chapter will cover why you might look for a new data system if your DSRP refuses to cooperate, shows a lack of regard for research-based best practices, and/or threatens to charge you for label changes or additions within the reporting environment. The "Work with Your DSRP" chapter will also cover reasons why you might nonetheless need a workaround in the meantime.

If you are sure "the best approach" shared earlier has not worked for you and you are up for this more tedious (and thus less desirable) approach, here are some tips to help you compensate for common labeling problems:

- **If report titles are poor** (e.g., confusing, inconsistent, or verbose), create an augmented report list or spreadsheet where you offer staff different descriptors (and other helpful information) for available reports. An excerpt from an augmented report list is shown below. Make this matrix easily accessible to staff and be sure they know where to find it.
- **If report titles are so specific that the number of available reports is overwhelming** (e.g., *Course Rosters with Math Test Scores Disaggregated to Include Only EL Students*), make something similar to the augmented report list (described earlier) that communicates report groupings. For example, you could indicate which five particular reports are all Course Roster lists, which eight particular reports are all Health Survey summaries, etc.

    This will help staff navigate the report list to find what they need without being overwhelmed by the number of options. Make this resource easily accessible to staff, as well.
- **If footers are not present on your reports,** or any available annotations do not adequately help users understand the data, adjust your augmented report list (described earlier) to include a "What You Need to Know" column. In this column, include one to three sentences for each report, offering the information most crucial to an educator being able to adequately understand, analyze, and use that particular report's data.

    Reference the 1.2 standards in the back of this book to craft helpful annotations. For now, the footers will not appear directly on reports (unless you run hard copies of reports through a printer or copy machine to add specific footers). Realistically, your best approach is to simply make your augmented report list readily available to staff and encourage them to reference it anytime they use a data report.

Time-Saving Resource

Use the OTCD *Label* Standards as a checklist as you craft any of your own reports' footers (to improve footer quality). See the 1.2 standards in the back of this book and on pages 1–2 online.

Report Title	Description	# of Years' Data	Multiple Students Listed	Multiple Teachers Listed	Multiple Subjects Listed	Multiple Schools Listed	Site Average Included	District Average Included	State Average Included	Contains Graphs or images
Percent Proficient Trend Analysis	Simple display of how student proficiency levels have gone up or down over time	2	X				X	X	X	X
Multi-Yr Performance Summary	One page per site, comparing the % of students within each proficiency band	3			X		X			X
Multiple Exam Listing	Teacher list with % of each teacher's students who scored Proficient on multiple tests	1		X			X	X		
Cluster Score Report	One page per class, listing each student's demographic & test data	1	X							

Figure 3.3 Sample Augmented Report List

However, provide these footers to your DSRP, as well. Since you have already done the work of writing a footer for each report, your DSRP's job of adding them directly to reports has just been made easier. Hopefully this will improve your DSRP's willingness to add them.

If You Provide Your Own Data System/Reports

If you provide your own data system and/or reports, you are in luck. You have direct control over when you add effective labels to your staff's reporting environment, and how. This section can also help if you provide just some of your own reports, such as building custom reports to supplement those your data system offers prebuilt.

The following steps and tools will help you add effective labels to your data reports:

1. Determine whether effective labels are, indeed, missing from your data reports. Referencing the *Label* standards in the back of this book can help.
2. Consult with key stakeholders at your district before working on new report labels. For example, your team of data coaches might provide feedback indicating a whole overhaul of existing reports is necessary, in which case you would not want to spend time adding footers to reports that should actually be replaced. It is also recommended you read this book in its entirety so you can prioritize changes.
3. Reference the "Label" chapter in *Designing Data Reports that Work: A Guide for Creating Data Systems in Schools and Districts*. The lessons in this chapter explain how to best implement each *Label* standard (offering specific examples, before and after illustrations, etc.). If you want a summary of research behind each *Label* standard, read the research information available.
4. Using the resources in the following box, implement labels that conform to specific OTCD Standards.

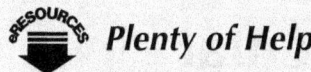 **Plenty of Help**

Your DSRP (or anyone else creating report titles and footers) can use:

- "Label" chapter in *Designing Data Reports that Work: A Guide for Creating Data Systems in Schools and Districts* (containing a lesson for implementing each OTCD Label standard).
- "Report Before and After Examples" file.

References

Hattie, J. (2010). Visibly learning from reports: The validity of score reports. *Online Educational Research Journal*. Retrieved from www.oerj.org/View?action=viewPaper&paper=6

James-Ward, C., Fisher, D., Frey, N., & Lapp, D. (2013). *Using data to focus instructional improvement*. Alexandra, VA: ASCD.

Metropolitan Life Insurance Company. (2013). *MetLife survey of the American teacher: Challenges for school leadership*. New York, NY: Author and Peanuts Worldwide.

Rankin, J. G. (2013). *Over-the-counter data's impact on educators' data analysis accuracy*. ProQuest Dissertations and Theses, 3575082. Retrieved from pqdtopen.proquest.com/doc/1459258514.html?FMT=ABS

U.S. Department of Education Office of Planning, Evaluation and Policy Development. (2009). *Implementing data-informed decision making in schools: Teacher access, supports and use*. United States Department of Education (ERIC Document Reproduction Service No. ED504191).

Zapata-Rivera, D., & VanWinkle, W. (2010). A research-based approach to designing and evaluating score reports for teachers. *ETS Research Memorandum. RM-10–01*. Princeton, NJ: ETS.

Supplemental Documentation

What Is Supplemental Documentation?

Effective labels are concise and do not overwhelm their readers. Yet using a high-stakes tool typically requires the conveyance of more information than can fit in a data report's title and footer. Again, we can see how the makers of over-the-counter medicine effectively resolve this dilemma. When a medication label is not large enough to accommodate all the information the consumer needs to use the contents properly, a folded-up piece of paper or pamphlet is enclosed within the package to offer further explanation on the product's use. The same is true of effective data reporting.

Data that is "over-the-counter" provides users with access to two types of supplemental documentation (accessible in printed and digital form):

- a **reference sheet**—often called an abstract—is a single page that accompanies a report in order to help the educator more easily understand the report (image shown later in this chapter).

- a **reference guide**—also called an interpretation guide—is a packet of two or more pages that accompanies a report in order to help the educator more easily use the report (images shown later in this chapter).

The reference sheet and reference guide help support educators of varied data analysis proficiency and comfort levels, as well as varied technical skills and comfort levels.

Why and How Should Supplemental Documentation Accompany Data?

Not all pertinent information about analyzing a particular report's data can fit in the report's title and label. Trying to cram in too much information would make report titles less effective and would make users less likely to read report footers. Too much information or text can overwhelm users and cause them to miss higher level implications (Hattie, 2010; VanWinkle, Vezzu, & Zapata-Rivera, 2011; Zapata-Rivera & VanWinkle, 2010).

Fortunately, data reporting environments can accompany data with supplementary documentation for each report, offering further explanation that typically cannot fit in the footer (covered in the previous chapter). This can be done with a reference sheet and/or reference guide. These offer report-specific details such as information about the test or data source, how to read the report, how to use it to answer essential questions, where to get more information, and more.

Reference Sheets

Research shows viewing a report's reference sheet before using the report can significantly improve chances of analyzing the report's data appropriately. The reference sheet is particularly helpful for the kinds of educators who want more support understanding a report and its data, but who do not have a lot of time and/or do not want to muddle through a lot of text (i.e., dislike reference guides, which are longer).

In the 211-educator Rankin (2013) study described earlier, where data analysis accuracy in the control group (without reference guides) was only 11 percent:

- Educators whose data reports were accompanied by reference sheets used the reference sheets 50 percent of the time.

> Reference sheets increase data analysis accuracy by 205–300 percent.

Tools

- In terms of relative and absolute differences, educators' data analyses were 205 percent more accurate (with a 12 percentage point difference) when a reference sheet was present and 300 percent more accurate (with a 22 percentage point difference) when respondents specifically indicated having used the reference sheet.

RESOURCES The reference sheets used in the Rankin (2013) study followed OTCD Standards covered in this book and match templates available online. Tested reference sheets included key content categories used to manage appropriate information:

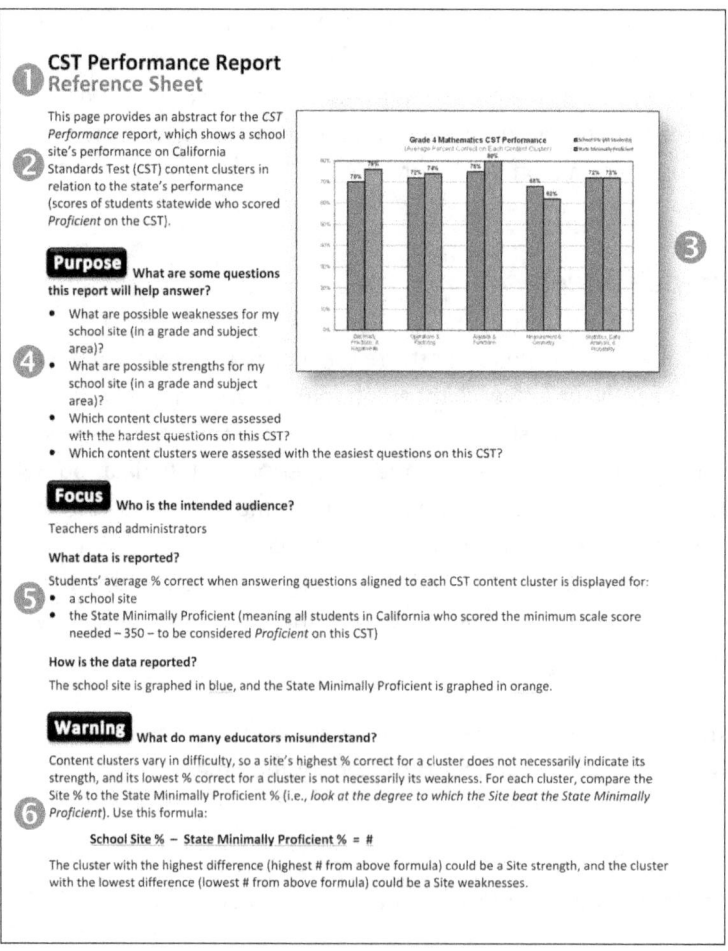

Figure 4.1

1. **Title** at the top of the reference sheet matches the title of the report. Notice how it is offset from the term *Reference Sheet* to reduce clutter around the title.

2. **Description** explains the sheet's purpose and any abbreviations (used in the report) for those who need them.

3. **Image** shows what the report typically looks like when it has been generated. If the report has multiple pages that look significantly different, they are included (it is fine to "stack" the images so only parts of subsequent report images show). This will help users know which report to use the sheet with, and in cases where they're viewing the reference sheet before generating the report it will help them decide if it's the report they want.

4. **Purpose** answers, "What are some questions this report will help answer?" After this follows a list of three to six specific, common questions users might have that this report is specifically designed to answer. Actual questions may be infinite, so this section tries to capture the most common, and users can look for questions similar or related to their own.

5. **Focus** addresses who the report is meant for and what data these users will see reported. This section provides answers to the questions, "Who is the intended audience?" "What data is reported?" and "How is the data reported?"

6. **Warning** is often the most important section of the sheet. It answers the question, "What do many educators misunderstand?" and can relate to mistakes they are most likely to make when analyzing this report's data, an inappropriate way in which educators often try to use this report's data, etc. Referencing pertinent Family Education Rights & Privacy Act (FERPA) regulations here can be helpful for some reports.

Given how busy educators are, they will only use (and thus benefit from) reference sheets if the sheets are easy to access. Given that 44 percent of educators use data systems directly for generating reports to analyze student data (Underwood, Zapata-Rivera, & VanWinkle, 2008), it is ideal to also make reference sheets available electronically, as well as printable and downloadable:

- Data systems or online/computerized collections of reports should offer an easy-to-spot link, which users can click while viewing a report, to immediately access the report's reference sheet.
- When viewing reference sheets on the computer/web, users should be able to download the sheets as Adobe PDF files (to save, email, etc.) and print them.

Reference Guides

Like reference sheets, research shows value in reference guides, which are like extended versions of the reference sheets. The reference guide is a two- or three-page guide (longer if necessary) that accompanies a report in order to help the educator more easily use the particular report and analyze its data. The guide is particularly helpful for the kind of educators who want extended help in using a report.

For example, while the reference sheet might tell users that a report *can* answer the question of, "Which school in my district showed the most improvement in Mathematics on the state test this year?" the reference guide will show exactly *how* to use the report to answer that particular question (e.g., where to look on the report, what pieces of data to compare there, what the implications are if a number there is red versus green, etc.). Reference guides provide more handholding for educators who need it, and they also provide deeper explanations for advanced users who want more specific details.

Reference guides are a good place for some of the research-based recommendations for information that should accompany reports. This is largely due to the need to avoid information overload within reports, though information should also be carefully selected for guides. Only information best suited for each report's guide should be included, based on a report's user's most likely needs.

In the 211-educator Rankin (2013) study described earlier, where data analysis accuracy in the control group (without reference guides) was only 11 percent:

- Educators whose data reports were accompanied by reference guides used the reference guides 52 percent of the time.
- In terms of relative and absolute differences, educators' data analyses were 273 percent more accurate (with a 19 percentage point difference) when a reference guide was present and 436 percent more accurate (with a 37 percentage point difference) when respondents specifically indicated having used the reference guide.

> Reference guides increase data analysis accuracy by 273–436 percent.

The reference guides used in the Rankin (2013) study followed OTCD Standards covered in this book and match templates available. Tested reference guides included key content categories used to manage appropriate information, please see Figures 4.2–4.4.

1. The same information included in the **reference sheet** (discussed in the previous section) should also constitute the first page of the reference guide. The data system could still offer the one-page reference sheet elsewhere in the system (e.g., a separate link) for those who only want that one page of information, but the reference sheet's content also functions well as the grounding information the reference guide needs. This way the two do not get separated (e.g., the reference sheet's information should not be left out of the reference guide with the expectation people will also access and view the reference sheet, because they often will not, and the result will be that people needing the extended help of the guide will be confused).
2. However, the guide's **heading** now clearly reads *Reference Guide* on its first page.
3. **Page Numbers** (e.g., *Pg. 1 of 3*) should be featured inobtrusively since reference guides are multiple pages. This will help users know if they are missing pages or if the pages get out of order, as can happen if the guide is printed and used as a handout.

CST Performance Report
Reference Guide

This 3-page guide explains the *CST Performance* report, which shows a school site's performance on California Standards Test (CST) content clusters in relation to the state's performance (scores of students statewide who scored *Proficient* on the CST).

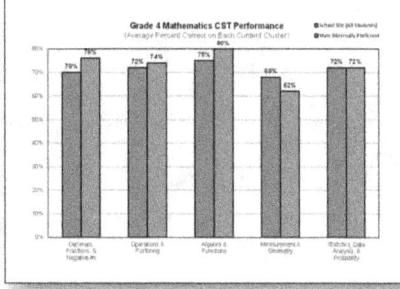

Purpose What are some questions this report will help answer?

- What are possible weaknesses for my school site (in a grade and subject area)?
- What are possible strengths for my school site (in a grade and subject area)?
- Which content clusters were assessed with the hardest questions on this CST?
- Which content clusters were assessed with the easiest questions on this CST?

Focus Who is the intended audience?

Teachers and administrators

What data is reported?

Students' average % correct when answering questions aligned to each CST content cluster is displayed for:
- a school site
- the State Minimally Proficient (meaning all students in California who scored the minimum scale score needed – 350 – to be considered *Proficient* on this CST)

How is the data reported?

The school site is graphed in blue, and the State Minimally Proficient is graphed in orange.

Warning What do many educators misunderstand?

Content clusters vary in difficulty, so a site's highest % correct for a cluster does not necessarily indicate its strength, and its lowest % correct for a cluster is not necessarily its weakness. For each cluster, compare the Site % to the State Minimally Proficient % (i.e., *look at the degree to which the Site beat the State Minimally Proficient*). Use this formula:

School Site % − State Minimally Proficient % = #

The cluster with the highest difference (highest # from above formula) could be a Site strength, and the cluster with the lowest difference (lowest # from above formula) could be a Site weaknesses.

Pg. 1 of 3

Figure 4.2

Supplemental Documentation

④ Instructions How do I read the report?

The bars show you the % of questions students answered correctly when answering questions aligned to each CST content cluster. %s above blue bars are results of students at the School Site, and %s above orange bars are results of students statewide who scored the minimum scale score needed (350) to be considered *Proficient* on this CST.

Example: The State Minimally Proficient students *and* the School Site's students both answered 72% of Qs correctly in this CST's *Statistics* cluster.

⑤ Essential Questions What are possible weaknesses for my school site (in a grade and subject area)?

Determine the cluster in which you most lagged behind the State Minimally Proficient's (SMP's) students (or beat them to the least degree). Since clusters vary in difficulty, SMP %s account for how easy or hard the clusters were. Use this formula:
  School % − SMP % = #

Example: For the *Decimals* cluster:
  School 70% − SMP 76% = −6

More than for any other cluster, Site did most poorly on the *Decimals* cluster (because of how Site compared to SMP). The *Decimals* cluster is most likely Site's weakness, even though the Site's 70% for *Decimals* was not its lowest %.

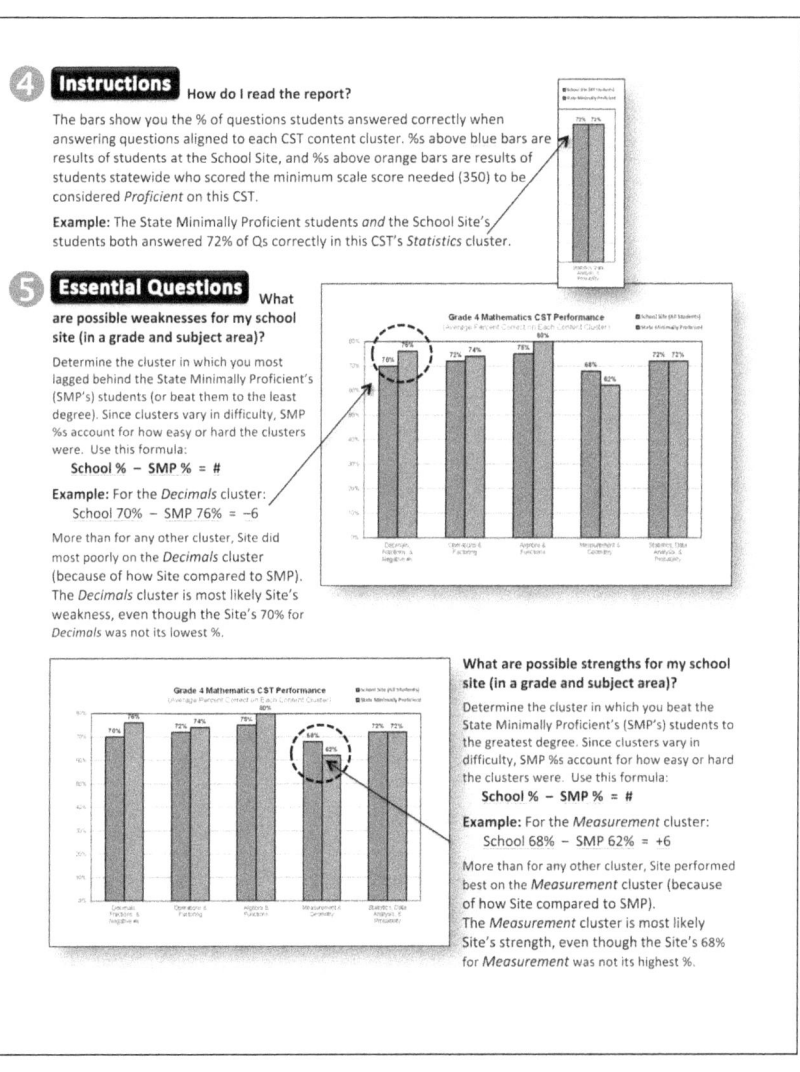

What are possible strengths for my school site (in a grade and subject area)?

Determine the cluster in which you beat the State Minimally Proficient's (SMP's) students to the greatest degree. Since clusters vary in difficulty, SMP %s account for how easy or hard the clusters were. Use this formula:
  School % − SMP % = #

Example: For the *Measurement* cluster:
  School 68% − SMP 62% = +6

More than for any other cluster, Site performed best on the *Measurement* cluster (because of how Site compared to SMP). The *Measurement* cluster is most likely Site's strength, even though the Site's 68% for *Measurement* was not its highest %.

Figure 4.3

Tools

Which content clusters were assessed with the hardest questions on this CST?

Find the State Minimally Proficient (SMP) lowest %. Since SMP %s are the average % of questions answered correctly by all students in California who scored the minimum scale score needed – 350 – to be considered *Proficient* on this CST, clusters they struggled with the most had the hardest questions.

Example: SMP's 62% in *Measurement* is lower than the 76%, 74%, 80%, and 72% SMP earned in the other clusters. Thus the *Measurement* cluster was likely assessed with the hardest questions.

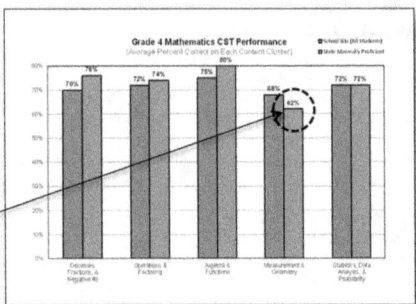

Which content clusters were assessed with the easiest questions on this CST?

Find the State Minimally Proficient (SMP) highest %. Clusters that SMP had the easiest time with had the easiest questions.

Example: SMP's 80% in *Algebra* is higher than the 76%, 74%, 62%, and 72% SMP earned in the other clusters. Thus the *Algebra* cluster was likely assessed with the easiest questions.

⑥ More Info Where can I find more info on the CST and its proper analysis?

Reference Chapter 1 of the *California Standardized Testing and Reporting (STAR) Post-Test Guide* at http://www.startest.org/archive.html.

Where can I find more info on analyzing CST content clusters?

Visit the Help system's *Data Analysis* manual.

Where can I learn how to generate this report in my data system?

Visit the Help system's *Reports* manual.

Figure 4.4

4. **Instructions** provide an answer to, "How do I read this report?", and then illustrate the explanation with an example.
5. **Essential Questions** walks the user through the process of how to use the report to answer each of the questions posed in the *Purpose* section of the first page. For example, the following provides users with guidance for each question:
    - The question is repeated in bold so it functions well as a subsection's heading and is easy to spot when users visually scan the sheet. Remember users will not necessarily want to use the report to answer every question the report is designed to answer. Many will have a particular question in mind and thus will skim the guide to use only information pertaining directly to that question.
    - An explanation is given for how the educator should use the report (e.g., where to look on the report and what to do with the data found there) to answer the given question.
    - The explanation is illustrated with snapshots of the report, arrows and circles to call attention to different areas, etc.
    - An example is given in Figure 4.3.
6. **More Info** shows the user how/where to get additional information on such topics as finding additional analysis guidance, and/or help generating this report in the data system. Many report users unnecessarily rely on other people to generate and print reports for them, whereas report-generating guidance could empower them.

The goal of the reference guide is not to teach the user about data analysis in general. For example, the importance of using multiple measures to make data-informed decisions is better suited for the help system, covered later in this book. Rather, a reference guide should only include information specific to the particular report with which it is paired. For example, supplemental documentation can address all important information that cannot fit within a report's footer, while also expounding upon the footer's brief statement(s) and upon information provided in the report's reference sheet.

Like reference sheets, the reference guides need to be easily accessible. While hard copies are helpful, the supplemental documentation must also be embedded within the data system so the relevant sheet and/or guide is one click away for the educator using a report.

Tools

Experience from the Field

"MNPS has approximately 10,000 staff serving over 82,000 students. We designed data guides for our district's data warehouse based off of Dr. Jenny Rankin's work (OTCD). I adapted them a bit for our needs, such as changing the name to data guide.

All information for the various sections of the data guides is gathered through a collaborative process. I start by creating a draft, and then I invite the necessary parties to a meeting to discuss the data guide and what needs to be in the guide. I meet with the departments that use the data the most and ask them to review and for input about the message they want conveyed throughout the district. The next draft is reviewed by the department and the data warehouse team before being disseminated. Each data guide is linked to its respective report.

Communication is disseminated throughout the district about the data guides through the monthly MNPS Data Spotlight Newsletter, which spotlights exemplary data use throughout the district and the availability of the latest data guide(s). We also have the information on our Intranet site.

The feedback from meeting with central office teams has been positive, as the data guide has facilitated us creating a common language about the data. It has also helped build capacity throughout the district to ensure that the data are used appropriately for making informed decisions that increase student achievement."

—Dr. Margie L. Johnson, Business Intelligence Coordinator
Metropolitan Nashville Public Schools

Over-the-Counter Data Standards

An ideal data reporting environment should reflect the OTCD *Supplemental Documentation* Standards, which stipulate research-based ways data systems/reports can provide reference sheets and reference guides. These standards can be found in the back of this book if you want to learn more about what qualifies as effective reference sheets and guides

> **Good News**
>
> You are likely not the one who has to implement these standards. You only need to know they exist so you can ask for them. If you do want advanced support creating your own supplemental documentation, read *Designing Data Reports that Work: A Guide for Creating Data Systems in Schools and Districts*.

However, you are likely not the one who has to implement these standards. This book you are reading is for educator leaders, but there is a second book out there written for data system/report providers. Those who design, program, manage, and provide the data system/reports you use (as well as educators who design or build some of their own data reports) can read *Designing Data Reports that Work: A Guide for Creating Data Systems in Schools and Districts* by Dr. Jenny Grant Rankin for help with the process of implementing every OTCD *Supplemental Documentation* Standard.

How to Get Supplemental Documentation

You do not need to have the ability to manipulate your data system in order to implement reference sheets and guides for your data reports. For example, if a third party (such as a vendor) provides your data system/reports, you can still create your own supplemental documentation and make it available to staff.

However, given your time constraints, the fastest and easiest way for you to get effective reference sheets and reference guides is to advocate for them. Since a third party data system/report provider (DSRP) typically serves multiple school districts, changes made at the DSRP level will benefit more educators and students than if the same changes are made only at the local level.

Tools

If Someone Other Than You Provides Your Data System

The Best Approach: The best way for you to get reference sheets and guides is to ask for them. This book provides an already-written email (shown on an upcoming page) you can send to your DSRP. Simply copy/paste text from the email's electronic copy into an email and modify/personalize your message as needed.

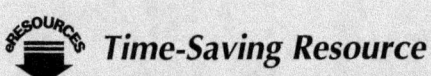 **Time-Saving Resource**

Copy/paste text from the following page's email into your own email.

Before you send the email:

1. Determine whether effective supplemental documentation is, indeed, missing from your data reports. Referencing the *Supplemental Documentation* standards in the back of this book can help you make this determination. Then you can enhance your email with details about specific problems you have noted.
2. Determine who at the DSRP is the best contact (this could be the Customer Service Department, but there is likely an implementation manager or other team member through whom you will find faster results).
3. Determine whether your district requires enhancement requests to go through a particular district administrator. In most cases it is appropriate for you to send the email yourself, but even then it is an advantage if district administrators *also* contact the DSRP advocating for effective reference sheets and reference guides.
4. It is also recommended you read this book in its entirety so you can prioritize requests you send to your DSRP.

See the "Work With Your DSRP" chapter for details on how this initial step can initiate change in your data system/reports. That chapter will also guide you if any follow-up is necessary.

Email to DSRP for Supplemental Documentation

Dear Data System/Report Provider,

I noticed our district's data system does not adhere to the Over-the-Counter Data *Supplemental Documentation* Standards that stipulate research-based ways to accompany education data reports with effective reference sheets and reference guides. Adherence to these *Supplemental Documentation* standards is necessary to best support educators' easy use and thorough understanding of reports' data. Consider:

- Only 48 percent of teachers' inferences based on given data are accurate at districts with strong data cultures (U.S. Department of Education Office of Planning, Evaluation and Policy Development, 2009), with other educators' analyses being less accurate.
- Educators' data analyses are 205 percent more accurate when a reference sheet accompanies a data report and 300 percent more accurate when respondents specifically indicate having used the reference sheet (Rankin, 2013).
- Educators' data analyses are 273 percent more accurate when a reference *guide* accompanies a data report and 436 percent more accurate (more than quadrupled!) when respondents specifically indicate having used the reference guide (Rankin, 2013).
- When they accompany data reports, educators use reference sheets 50 percent of the time and use reference guides 52 percent of the time (Rankin, 2013).

Please attune our data system/reports to adhere to the research-based Over-the-Counter Data *Supplemental Documentation* Standards. These resources can help you:

Tools

- Over-the-Counter Data Standards are available with other eResources (including details on the research behind each standard) at wwww.routledge.com/9781138956155 (the *Supplemental Documentation* standards are on pages 2–3).

- Free templates (for reference sheets and reference guides) that are aligned to Over-the-Counter Data Standards and the supplemental documentation shown to be effective in the Rankin study are also available at wwww.routledge.com/9781138956155.

- Read the book *Designing Data Reports that Work: A Guide for Creating Data Systems in Schools and Districts*, by Dr. Jenny Grant Rankin. This guide explains how to implement each reporting standard within a data system/report (offering specific examples, illustrations, etc.).

Thank you very much for your time and assistance. Adhering to these standards will offer tremendous help to educators and students.

—Me

Rankin, J. G. (2013). *Over-the-counter data's impact on educators' data analysis accuracy.* ProQuest Dissertations and Theses, 3575082. Retrieved from www.pqdtopen.proquest.com/doc/14592 58514.html?FMT=ABS

U.S. Department of Education Office of Planning, Evaluation and Policy Development. (2009). *Implementing data-informed decision making in schools: Teacher access, supports and use.* United States Department of Education (ERIC Document Reproduction Service No. ED504191).

The Less Desirable Approach: Ideally your DSRP will comply with the email you sent in the previous ("The Best Approach") section so you and your staff can benefit from supplemental documentation. This book's "Work with Your DSRP" chapter will cover why you might look for a new data system if your DSRP refuses to cooperate, shows a lack of regard for research-

Supplemental Documentation

based best practices, and/or threatens to charge you for the supplemental documentation's creation or use. The "Work With Your DSRP" chapter will also cover reasons why you might nonetheless need a workaround in the meantime. Thus, if you are sure "the best approach" shared earlier has not worked for you and you are up for this more tedious (and thus less desirable) approach, here are some tips to help you compensate for common supplemental documentation problems:

- **If no reference sheets and/or guides are available** (meaning your DSRP does not offer supplemental documentation in any form and neither does your school district), you can create these tools. Reference bullets 1–5 in the next section ("If You Provide Your Own Data System") offer guidance.

    After creating supplemental documentation for reports, your next step will be to advocate for the documentation's inclusion in your data system. Read the next bullet for assistance.

- **If guides are available but not within the data system** (meaning your DSRP has guides available to email you, or a district administrator has them stored as documents on her computer, but there are no report-to-documentation links within the data system), you will want to encourage your DSRP to give educators more direct report-to-documentation access. Following guidelines in the previous ("The Best Approach") section, contact your DSRP about adding such access, perhaps sending an email similar to that provided. However, make it clear that the supplemental documentation already exists (e.g., share it with your district's consent if your district's staff created it). Since sheets or guides have already been created, your DSRP's job of simply storing these within the data system and adding report-to-documentation links is not as hard.

    If your DSRP will not house the sheets or guides directly within your data system, you will want to house them somewhere easily accessible by all staff. A staff portal within your district website works well, as you can arrange the Adobe PDF files in a logical order and train staff to access them when using the data system's reports. An online help system (covered in the next chapter) is also an effective place to house the documentation.

Tools

If You Provide Your Own Data System

If you provide your own data system, you have direct control over when and how you embed supplemental documentation within your staff's reporting environment. The following steps and tools will help you add supplemental documentation to your data reporting environment:

1. Determine whether reference sheets and reference guides are, indeed, missing from your data system. Referencing the *Supplemental Documentation* standards in the back of this book can help.

2. Consult with key stakeholders at your district before working on new supplemental documentation. For example, a principal might reveal one of her grade level chairs has already created similar guides for her colleagues, in which case you would not have to start from scratch. A team approach can also lighten your workload and help you determine where best to start (e.g., with sheets rather than guides, for particular reports first, etc.). It is also recommended you read this book in its entirety so you can prioritize efforts.

3. Access the free templates (for reference sheets and reference guides) that are aligned to OTCD Standards and were shown to be effective in the Rankin (2013) study. These are available in various formats (so you can choose which you like best, as formats tested equally effectively).

4. Reference the "Supplemental Documentation" chapter in *Designing Data Reports that Work: A Guide for Creating Data Systems in Schools and Districts*. The lessons in this chapter explain how to best implement each *Supplemental Documentation* standard (offering specific examples, before and after illustrations, etc.). If you want a summary research behind each *Supplemental Documentation* standard, read the research information available.

5. Using the above resources, implement supplemental documentation that conforms to specific OTCD Standards.

Supplemental Documentation

Plenty of Help

Your DSRP (or anyone else creating reference sheets and reference guides) can use:

-  Free templates for reference sheets and reference guides
- Samples of reference sheets and reference guides used by others
- "Supplemental Documentation" chapter in *Designing Data Reports that Work: A Guide for Creating Data Systems in Schools and Districts* (containing a lesson for implementing each OTCD Supplemental Documentation standard).

References

Hattie, J. (2010). Visibly learning from reports: The validity of score reports. *Online Educational Research Journal.* Retrieved from www.oerj.org/View?action=viewPaper&paper=6

Rankin, J. G. (2013). *Over-the-counter data's impact on educators' data analysis accuracy.* ProQuest Dissertations and Theses, 3575082. Retrieved from pqdtopen.proquest.com/doc/1459258514.html?FMT=ABS

Underwood, J. S., Zapata-Rivera, D., & VanWinkle, W. (2008) Growing pains: Teachers using and learning to use IDMS®. *ETS Research Memorandum. RM-08–07.* Princeton, NJ: ETS.

U.S. Department of Education Office of Planning, Evaluation and Policy Development. (2009). *Implementing data-informed decision making in schools: Teacher access, supports and use.* United States Department of Education (ERIC Document Reproduction Service No. ED504191).

VanWinkle, W., Vezzu, M., & Zapata-Rivera, D. (2011). Question-based reports for policymakers. *ETS Research Memorandum. RM-11–16.* Princeton, NJ: ETS.

Zapata-Rivera, D., & VanWinkle, W. (2010). A research-based approach to designing and evaluating score reports for teachers (*ETS Research Memorandum. RM-10–01*). Princeton, NJ: ETS.

5 Help System

What Is a Help System?

Remember our example of making something easy to use by making it "over-the-counter." Every year, approximately 50 million different people use WebMD (the WebMD Health Network, found at www.WebMD.com) (Kronstadt, Moiduddin, & Sellheim, 2009). Even when medication features effective labeling and supplemental documentation, its users still crave the convenience of an online help system where they can run searches, explore topics, and find answers to their questions. The same is true of data system users.

Data that is "over-the-counter" provides users with an online help system containing two types of lessons:

- **Technical lessons** illustrate how to use the data system or other technical reporting tools (e.g., what to click for various tasks); these lessons are generally task-based and are somewhat common in data reporting environments.
- **Data analysis lessons** communicate key data analysis topics and practices (e.g., how to determine statistical significance); these lessons are generally topic-based and are rare in data reporting environments.

The lessons offer support to educators of varied technical and data proficiency levels, particularly when they are alone (such as working from home). Lessons can also be used in conjunction with formalized PD.

Why and How Should a Help System Accompany Data?

My mother is a brilliant woman. However, like many educators using data reports and data systems, most of her life was lived during a time when personal computers did not exist.

When my mother got her first computer, I would sit down with her to guide her in how to turn it on, view a document, and then turn the computer off. The goal was to also show her how to do more, but she would get so overwhelmed by the lesson of turning the computer on and off (which button to press, where to find it, etc.), feverishly taking notes on everything I said, that it took a week of nightly lessons (adjusting to her needs just as I would adjust for younger students) before she was ready to conquer another task.

At the end of the week, my mother was beaming as she had accomplished the task of turning on the computer and viewing a document with very little help. It was then time to turn off the computer. She looked at me nervously and said, "The *Start* button?" as this task was accomplished by clicking the *Start* button and then clicking *Shut Down*.

"Yes!" I gushed. Then this accomplished academic did something that had never been a part of any of our lessons. She looked at the monitor (an old-school monitor—not a fancy, touchscreen kind), and she pressed the *Start* button on her monitor with her finger. That's right: she pressed it *with her finger*, not her mouse's cursor.

Educators are familiar with the term *emotional filter*. It's something we refer to when an English Learner (EL) student hears foreign words in the classroom, and the anxiety of encountering something unfamiliar causes him or her to doubt his or her abilities. An internal, emotional filter can arise that interferes with the student's ability to learn things he or she would otherwise have no problems learning. It's like getting so nervous during a job interview that you do not register what question your potential boss just asked you.

When my mother pressed the monitor with her finger, she had not lost her wits. Rather, her emotional filter had been up each time we used the computer, because she was highly intimidated by technology. Terms like *icon, cursor,* and *double-click* that others do not think twice about further exacerbated her fears, even when they were explained, because they were unfamiliar. My mother was out of her comfort zone.

Some data system users are doubly cursed by their emotional filters. Many are intimidated by data analysis and use, and many are *also* intimidated by technology. Thus avid users of data and technology cannot wisely assume that what they consider to be a user-friendly data system will be perceived that way by all educators. Likewise, they cannot assume data analyses they perform with ease will be as easy for others.

If you ever doubt this, remember the brilliant woman who tried to use an old-school monitor like a touchscreen. Over a third of educators are older than 50 and nearing retirement (Papay, Harvard Graduate School of Education, 2007). Though some of these may nonetheless be data system power users, computer technology was not likely part of their upbringing and they may struggle like my mother. Young teachers can also be technologically challenged. Educators of all technology comfort levels could still struggle when it comes to using technology specifically for data needs, as intelligent as these professionals are.

In addition, most educators analyze data alone even when there are staff members who can help (USDEOPEPD, 2009). This means even when staff resources such as data coaches and statisticians are available, educators analyzing a report's data are likely to be doing so without these people's help at times. Since most data systems are moving in the direction of being online, educators access and use them outside of the classroom, such as at home in the evening or in a coffee shop on the weekend.

> A shorter, targeted manual or user-friendly help system causes users to need 40 percent less training time and to successfully complete 50 percent more tasks.
>
> —van der Meij, 2008

It is thus crucial that any data reporting environment includes a help system component that serves as a virtual coach. Ideally this is built into a data system, accessible through an easy-to-spot link. However, it can also be housed outside the data system (yet still online) when a within-system link is not possible. In either case, users should be able to easily download each lesson as an Adobe PDF file and print each lesson if needed.

With easy access to both technical and data analysis lessons, educators analyzing data alone will not be completely alone, as a tech expert's guidance and data expert's guidance will be in the room with them. These experts' guidance will support educators in using the data system and facilitate data analyses with which the educator wants help.

Remember: we should not be content to merely give educators data; rather, we should do as much as we can to ensure educators' analyses of that data are *accurate*. The help system is a crucial tool for making data work for educators. A shorter, targeted manual or user-friendly help system causes users to need 40 percent less training time and to successfully complete 50 percent more tasks (Hattie, 2010; van der Meij, 2008).

Tech Lessons (Using the System)

A survey of 600 K-12 teachers revealed 50 percent of teachers report inadequate support for using technology in the classroom, and 46 percent report they lack the training needed to use technology successfully to help students (Piehler, 2014). In addition, teachers' awareness or perceptions about a data system's available infrastructure and capabilities is not in line with the actual available infrastructure; for example, statistics suggest fewer teachers believe they have access to students' performance on diagnostic tests than teachers who actually do have such access (Faria et al., 2012).

Educators cannot view data reports on their own to analyze data in a data system if they do not know how to access the reports, generate the reports, etc. Ideally, a data system should be intuitive enough that users rarely have to turn to the help system for guidance. However, *intuitive* is a subjectively applied term. Lack of tech-familiarity can cause users to struggle with systems others find easy to use. Lessons on using the system should be available in all key cases where help is needed.

Thus a help system should contain tech lessons that help educators complete tasks within the data system. Think of these lessons as a virtual tech coach or trainer who can assist educators in using the system when a live person who can help is not present.

Illustrated, step-by-step tech lessons should be present for all common technical tasks and key technical topics. Following are just some of the key technical lessons you might want to house in your data system or reporting environment, based on which are applicable. These lessons are

Tools

> ### *Sample Tech Lessons (Categorized)*
>
> Introduction
>
> - Log in and Out
> - Change Password
> - Use the System (Overview)
>
> Prebuilt Reports
>
> - Find a Report
> - Generate a Report
> - Download/Print a Report
>
> Training Tools
>
> - Videos
> - Trainer Toolkit (support for educators training other educators)

just a start, and you will also want sets of lessons for other parts of your system. For example, collections of lessons that impact data reporting might include:

- **data administrator** (a set of lessons only for educators who help manage the report environment, such as by loading the data it displays);
- **custom reports** (sorting, creating, sharing, editing, finding, etc.);
- **dashboard** (customizing, using, etc.);
- **assessments** (scanning, using item banks, taking online tests, creating, sharing, editing, finding, etc.);
- **student groups** (creating, sharing, selecting to generate a report for the group, etc.);
- **gradebook** and report cards, etc.

Data Analysis Lessons

The American Association of School Administrators (AASA) reports teachers know data can help them but are overwhelmed by the data and need help using it (Stansbury, 2013). Most education professionals are not data-savvy and they need help understanding and interpreting data before they can make correctly informed decisions (SAS Institute, 2013). In fact, stakeholders at *all* levels have trouble interpreting data (Underwood, Zapata-Rivera, & VanWinkle, 2010). Odendahl (2011) noted something as complex as test scores cannot be understood without a user's manual.

A help system should contain lessons that help educators analyze data in the reporting environment. These are the types of lessons most frequently missing from data systems, but they are also the lessons most likely to improve the accuracy of educators' data analyses. Think of the help system's data analysis lessons as a virtual data coach or trainer who can assist educators in appropriately using data when a live person who can help is not present.

Even more so than for the technical lessons, the data analysis lessons in a help system should be written by a reporting expert such as yourself who is well-versed in region-specific data use. A team of knowledgeable educators offering to contribute can also be enlisted (with gratitude), as long as they all adhere to the same guidelines, particularly those pertaining to the lessons' consistency. This book's upcoming "How to Get a Help System" section will help.

Data analysis lessons should be present for all common analysis tasks and key topics. Below is an example of lesson types (e.g., "Data Analysis" manual chapters) appropriate for the data analysis help system component:

- **Definitions** (e.g., Abbreviations, Performance Band, Proficiency Level, Raw Score, Scale Score, Subgroup, etc.);
- **Accountability and Requirements** (e.g., Common Core State Standards FAQ; APR: Understanding API, AYP, PI, etc.; AMAOs and Title III Accountability, etc.);
- **Test-Specific** Analyses (e.g., Test Program A: Understanding Scores; Test Program B: Appropriate Grade Level Analysis; Test Program B: Appropriate Content Cluster Analyses; Test Program B: Performance Level Cut Points, etc.);

Tools

- Popular **Approaches to Data Use** (e.g., Student Grouping, Essential Questions, Data Dialogues, Start of the Year Data Use, Use Data to Differentiate Instruction, etc.);
- Using the System for **Response to Intervention** (RTI) (e.g., Why Use [the Data System] for RTI?, Good Instruction, Regularly Assess Students, Analyze Assessment Results to Determine Student Needs, Tiered Instruction and Intervention, Evaluate RTI Outcomes, Parent Involvement, and Student Involvement);
- **Resources** (Conference Presentations and Handouts, Assessment Design, etc.).

Over-the-Counter Data Standards

An ideal data reporting environment should reflect the OTCD *Help System* Standards, which stipulate the research-based ways data systems can provide technical lessons and data analysis lessons. These standards can be found in the back of this book if you want to learn more about what qualifies as effective help lessons.

> ### Good News
>
> You are likely not the one who has to implement these standards. You only need to know they exist so you can ask for them. If you do want advanced support creating your own help system, read *Designing Data Reports that Work: A Guide for Creating Data Systems in Schools and Districts.*

However, you are likely not the one who has to implement these standards. This book you are reading is for educator leaders, but there is a second book out there written for data system/report providers. Those who design, program, manage, and provide the data system/reports you use (as well as educators who design or build some of their own data reports) can read *Designing Data Reports that Work: A Guide for Creating Data Systems in*

Schools and Districts by Dr. Jenny Grant Rankin for help with the process of implementing every OTCD *Help System* Standard.

> ### Experience from the Field
>
> "Before our selection of a help desk system we struggled with publishing, maintaining, and allowing users to find our help documents. We used tools like Microsoft Word to create documents, and often we would convert them to PDFs. Then we would attach them and send them out in emails. Sometimes we would post the documents but they weren't searchable.
>
> Our users were relying on these documents that sometimes they would print. The static nature of these documents was not agile enough to keep up with the changes in the software tools we were using. We decided we had a need to research and select a new system for assisting our users.
>
> We chose a system called ScreenSteps because it allowed us to quickly publish help-related documents that were searchable. These documents could be updated quickly. One of the issues we had with our other documents was versioning. This new system allowed our help document creators to check out any help document and then edit it and republish the document. Instead of having static documents our help desk became more alive and vibrant. We were able to quickly make minor changes to documents when new versions of our software arrived."
>
> —Mike Morrison, Chief Technology Officer
> Laguna Beach Unified School District

How to Get a Help System

You do not need to have the ability to manipulate your data system in order to implement a help system. For example, if a third party (such as a vendor) provides your data system/reports, you can still create your own help system and make it available to staff.

However, given your time constraints, the fastest and easiest way for you to get a help system is to advocate for it. Since a third party data system/report provider (DSRP) typically serves multiple school districts, an addition of a help system at the DSRP level will benefit more educators and students than if a help system is only added at the local level.

If Someone Other Than You Provides Your Data System

The Best Approach: The best way for you to get a comprehensive help system is to ask for it. This book provides an already-written email (shown on an upcoming page) you can send to your DSRP. Simply copy/paste text from the email's electronic copy into an email, and modify/personalize your message as needed.

> ### *Time-Saving Resource*
>
> Copy/paste text from the following page's email into your own email.

Before you send the email:

1. Determine whether an effective help system is, indeed, missing from your data system. Referencing the *Help System* standards in the back of this book can help you make this determination. Then you can enhance your email with details about specific problems you have noted.
2. Determine who at the DSRP is the best contact (this could be the Customer Service Department, but there is likely an implementation manager or other team member through whom you will find faster results).
3. Determine whether your district requires enhancement requests to go through a particular district administrator. In most cases it is appropriate for you to send the email yourself, but even then it is an advantage if district administrators *also* contact the DSRP advocating for effective help lessons.

Email to DSRP for Help System

Dear Data System/Report Provider,

I noticed our district's data system does not adhere to the Over-the-Counter Data *Help System* Standards that stipulate research-based ways to accompany education data reports with an online, searchable help system. Such a help system should contain task-based lessons on how to use the data system (e.g., where to click to generate a report), *and also* topic-based lessons to help educators use the data (e.g., using multiple measures). Adherence to these *Help System* standards is necessary to best support educators' easy use of the data system and thorough understanding of reports' data. Consider:

- Only 48 percent of teachers' inferences based on given data are accurate at districts with strong data cultures (U.S. Department of Education Office of Planning, Evaluation and Policy Development, 2009), with other educators' analyses being less accurate.
- Technology-related problems can impede teachers' ability to analyze test data properly, and translating data into action is complex; educators can only effectively use data analysis tools if they receive ongoing support (Rennie Center for Education Research and Policy, 2006).
- Teachers have difficulty using data systems due to varying technological sophistication levels when it comes to using the data system to interpret student data, even among teachers who serve as assessment coaches to their peers (Underwood, Zapata-Rivera, & VanWinkle, 2008).
- A shorter, targeted manual or user-friendly help system causes users to need 40 percent less training time and to successfully complete 50 percent more tasks than would be accomplished with only access to a full-sized manual (van der Meij, 2008).

Please attune our data system/reports to adhere to the research-based Over-the-Counter Data *Help System* Standards. These resources can help you:

Tools

- Over-the-Counter Data Standards are available with other eResources (including details on the research behind each standard) at www.routledge.com/products/9781138956155 (the *Help System* standards are on pages 4–5).
- Products like ScreenSteps (www.ScreenSteps.com) make it simple to create a help system that is illustrated, step-by-step, searchable, well-organized, downloadable/printable, inexpensive, and easy to access online.
- Read the book *Designing Data Reports that Work: A Guide for Creating Data Systems in Schools and Districts,* by Dr. Jenny Grant Rankin. This guide explains how to implement each reporting standard within a data system/report (offering specific examples, illustrations, etc.).

Thank you very much for your time and assistance. Adhering to these standards will offer tremendous help to educators and students.

—Me

Rennie Center for Education Research and Policy. (February, 2006). *Data-driven teaching: Tools and trends.* Cambridge, MA: Rennie Center for Education Research and Policy.

Underwood, J. S., Zapata-Rivera, D., & VanWinkle, W. (2008). Growing pains: Teachers using and learning to use IDMS®. *ETS Research Memorandum. RM-08-07.* Princeton, NJ: ETS.

U.S. Department of Education Office of Planning, Evaluation and Policy Development. (2009). *Implementing data-informed decision making in schools: Teacher access, supports and use.* United States Department of Education (ERIC Document Reproduction Service No. ED504191).

Van der Meij, H. (2008). Designing for user cognition and affect in a manual. Should there be special support for the latter? *Learning & Instruction, 18*(1), 18–29.

4. It is also recommended you read this book in its entirety so you can prioritize requests you send to your DSRP.

See the "Work With Your DSRP" chapter for details on how this initial step can initiate change in your data system.

The Less Desirable Approach: Ideally your DSRP will comply with the email you sent in the previous ("The Best Approach") section so you and your staff can benefit from a comprehensive help system. This book's "Work With Your DSRP" chapter will cover why you might look for a new data system if your DSRP refuses to cooperate, shows a lack of regard for research-based best practices, and/or threatens to charge you for the help system's creation or use. The "Work With Your DSRP" chapter will also cover reasons why you might nonetheless need a workaround in the meantime. Thus, if you are sure "the best approach" shared earlier has not worked for you and you are up for this more tedious (and thus less desirable) approach, here are some tips to help you compensate for common help system problems:

- **If no help system is available** (meaning your DSRP does not offer a help system in any form and neither does your school district), you can create one. Reference bullets 1–5 in the next section ("If You Provide Your Own Data System") offer guidance. Also ask your DSRP for any assorted lessons it might have (e.g., many DSRPs have "how to" sheets they hand out at trainings yet do not house online) to make this task easier. Try to get electronic copies of these so you can copy/paste content as permitted.

    After creating a help system for your reporting environment, your next step will be to advocate for an ever-present "Help" link to be embedded in your data system so users can click the link to be taken straight to your help system. Read the "If a help system is available but not within the data system" bullet for assistance.

- **If a help system is available, but it is missing some important lessons** (e.g., there is no "How to Edit an Existing Assessment" lesson, and your staff often struggles with this task), you can advocate for the lessons' inclusion. Email your DSRP in the manner explained earlier, only make it clear which lessons are missing and why they are important. If you have any non-copyrighted materials to help (e.g., if a "Conduct a Data

Dialogue" lesson is missing from the help system and you have a set of data dialogue instructions and a graphic organizer you regularly use with staff), provide these to your DSRP to use within its help system, providing written consent as appropriate.

Sometimes a large number of important lessons are missing. For example, when help systems are featured for data systems, they typically include tech lessons but no data analysis lessons. In this case, your best option is to advocate for the lesson type's inclusion (in the same way covered in the previous "The Best Approach" section).

If that approach fails and you are considering the sizeable (and thus less desirable) task of creating your own lessons of that type, work with your DSRP to see if you can gain access to create the lessons directly within its existing help system. You might even be able to garner free training or a discount from your DSRP in exchange for any work you undertake on the DSRP's behalf. If you create lessons outside of the help system, work with your DSRP to offer the content directly within its help system.

- **If a help system is available but not within the data system** (meaning you or your DSRP offers a help system, but there is no ever-present "Help" link within the data system that leads to the help system), you will want to encourage your DSRP to give educators more direct help system access. Following guidelines in the previous ("The Best Approach") section, contact your DSRP about adding such access, perhaps sending an email similar to that provided in this chapter. However, make it clear that the help system already exists (e.g., share it with your district's consent if your district created it). Since lessons have already been created, your DSRP's job of simply storing these within the data system and adding a "Help" link is not as hard.

If your DSRP will not house a help system link within your data system, you will want to house it somewhere easily accessible by all staff. For example, place the link on the staff portal's opening page within your district website and train staff to access it when using the data system or its data.

If You Provide Your Own Data System

If you provide your own data system, you have direct control over when and how you embed a help system within your staff's reporting environment. The following steps and tools will help you create a help system and add a "Help" link within your data reporting environment:

1. Determine whether an effective help system is, indeed, missing from your data system. Referencing the *Help System* standards in the back of this book can help.

2. Consult with key stakeholders at your district before working on a help system. For example, a data coach might share a packet of lessons she created for use when coaching staff, in which case you would not have to start from scratch; rather, you could copy some of the content and place it within lessons you create using a help system creation tool such as ScreenSteps). A team approach can also lighten your workload and help you determine where best to start (e.g., with tech lesson basics, then data analysis basics, then more advanced tech tasks, etc.). It is also recommended you read this book in its entirety so you can best prioritize your efforts.

3. Also consult with key stakeholders at your district when selecting a help system creation tool like ScreenSteps (www.ScreenSteps.com). Note the author of this book is not affiliated with ScreenSteps in any way; rather, I am a fan and user of the product. Such a tool will best allow you to conform to the *Help System* standards, as you will be able to create successful lessons quickly and easily in a format that will allow users to run searches for lessons, export lessons to PDF, view an illustration for every step, etc. It will also be easy for you to manage lessons and make quick changes when necessary. Creating static lessons using a document program like Microsoft Word will not render the same results.

4. Reference the "Help System" chapter in *Designing Data Reports that Work: A Guide for Creating Data Systems in Schools and Districts*. The lessons in this chapter explain how to best implement each *Help System* standard (offering specific examples, before and after illustrations, etc.). If you want a summary of research behind each *Help System* standard, read the research information available.

Tools

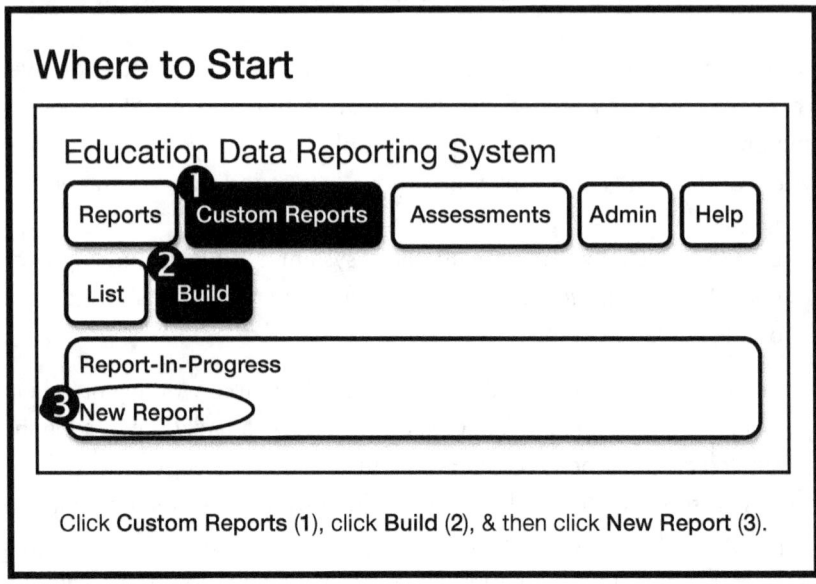

Figure 5.1 Illustrated Step Within a Lesson

Plenty of Help

Your DSRP (or anyone else creating help lessons) can use:

- "Help System" chapter in *Designing Data Reports that Work: A Guide for Creating Data Systems in Schools and Districts* (containing a lesson for implementing each OTCD Help System standard).

5. Using the above resources, implement a help system that conforms to specific OTCD Standards.

References

Faria, A., Heppen, J., Li, Y., Stachel, S., Jones, W., Sawyer, K., Thomsen, K., Kutner, M., Miser, D., Lewis, S., Casserly, M., Simon, C., Uzzell, R., & Corcoran, A., Palacios, M. (2012, Summer). *Charting success: Data use and student achievement in urban schools.* Council of the Great City Schools and the American Institutes for Research. Retrieved from www.cgcs.org/cms/lib/DC00001581/Centricity/Domain/87/Charting_Success.pdf

Hattie, J. (2010). Visibly learning from reports: The validity of score reports. *Online Educational Research Journal.* Retrieved from www.oerj.org/View?action=viewPaper&paper=6

Kronstadt, J., Moiduddin, A., & Sellheim, W. (2009, March). *Consumer use of computerized applications to address health and health care needs: Prepared for U.S. Department of Health and Human Services, Office of the Secretary, Assistant Secretary for Planning and Evaluation.* Bethesda, MD: NORC at the University of Chicago.

Odendahl, N. V. (2011). *Testwise: Understanding educational assessment, Volume 1.* Lanham, MD: Rowman & Littlefield Education.

Papay, J., Harvard Graduate School of Education. (2007). *Aspen Institute datasheet: The teaching workforce.* Washington, DC: The Aspen Institute.

Piehler, C. (2014, March 10). Survey finds 50 percent of K-12 teachers get inadequate support for using technology in the classroom. *T/H/E Journal.* Retrieved from thejournal.com/articles/2014/03/10/digedu-survey-results.aspx

Rennie Center for Education Research and Policy. (2006, February). *Data-driven teaching: Tools and trends.* Cambridge, MA: Rennie Center for Education Research and Policy.

SAS Institute. (2013). *Best practices in information management, reporting and analytics for education.* Retrieved from www.fs24.formsite.com/edweek/form15/secure_index.html

Stansbury, M. (2013, July). Nine templates to help educators leverage school data: New industry collaborative says using data effectively can help close education gaps. *eSchool News.* Retrieved from www.eschoolnews.com/2013/01/07/nine-templates-to-help-educators-leverage-school-data/?ast=104&astc=9990

Underwood, J. S., Zapata-Rivera, D., & VanWinkle, W. (2008). Growing pains: Teachers using and learning to use IDMS®. *ETS Research Memorandum. RM-08–06*. Princeton, NJ: ETS.

Underwood, J. S., Zapata-Rivera, D., & VanWinkle, W. (2010). An evidence-centered approach to using assessment data for policymakers. *ETS Research Report. RR-10–03*. Princeton, NJ: ETS.

U.S. Department of Education Office of Planning, Evaluation and Policy Development. (2009). *Implementing data-informed decision making in schools: Teacher access, supports and use*. United States Department of Education (ERIC Document Reproduction Service No. ED504191).

Van der Meij, H. (2008). Designing for user cognition and affect in a manual. Should there be special support for the latter? *Learning & Instruction, 18*(1), 18–29.

Package/Display

What Is Package/Display?

You would never consume medicine that was packaged in a way that lacked credibility (e.g., the label contained spelling errors) or featured poor design (e.g., the box showed childlike images implying the medicine was for children when it was actually only for adults). Fortunately, over-the-counter products adhere to better standards. Likewise, data system users should not be expected to consume data that is poorly packaged and displayed.

Data that is "over-the-counter" is presented to users with package/display that:

- maintains **credibility** through secure, error-free data and displays;
- contains **key features** like summaries and calculations, vital data, appropriate graphs, and clear headers;
- employs effective **design** practices;
- offers efficient **navigation**;
- provides useful **input controls** (please see Figure 6.1), which allow users to customize reports.

Improved package/display within a data system and its reports contributes to easier data system use, easier data use, and more accurate data use.

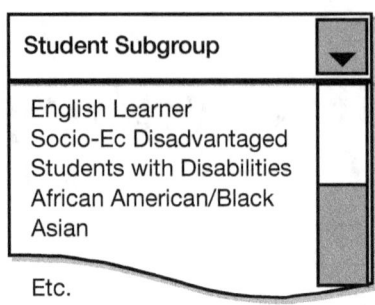

Figure 6.1

Why and How Should Data Be Packaged/Displayed Effectively?

Consider this question:

> What's your ultimate goal when you use an oven?

You're likely baking something in hopes it will taste good. If an oven looked beautiful, used the latest technology, cooked your food faster than a speeding bullet, was easy to use, and had all kinds of ancillary options like a built-in timer and cleaning genie, but *any food that was baked in this oven came out tasting like cardboard* . . . would you consider it a good oven?

I'm guessing your answer is *no*. Of course this would not be a good oven. Even if you assigned a rubric for each category, giving it a top score for appearance, technological innovation, speed, user-friendliness, and ancillary options, its score in the final product—how the food comes out—should trump all the other categories in your evaluation of the oven's worth. The end result is the most important attribute of the oven, because it is the entire reason you are using the oven.

Now consider this question:

> Why did you (or your district) buy a data system or other reporting tool?

You likely hoped your data system and reports would be easy to use, employ the latest technology, be capable of handling large quantities of longitudinal data, and budget-conscious, but what was the main thing you hoped to get out of it? Your answer is likely along the lines of *feedback*. A data system's main purpose is feedback to help educators help students. It is the whole reason you're putting all that data into the system and training staff to use it in the first place.

If the feedback that comes out of the data system does not function well—e.g., if the reports poorly package/display the data so the accuracy of educators' data analyses is hurt rather than helped—is it a good data system? No. . . . but it could be if these report designs were fixed.

Most data reports that educators analyze come from data systems of one form or another; these reports are a data system's main means of communicating feedback. It takes programmers to make the reports available in the systems, but often educators and report design experts are left out of the process. Not every programmer sees this as a problem, but experts in the field recognize this as a grave problem. This is because education and report design are not simple matters.

The design of an education data report (such as a student data report) can make or break its users' ability to understand the data, draw accurate conclusions, and respond appropriately. This means the design of a data report impacts students.

Credibility

If you picked a package of over-the-counter medicine off the shelf and noticed its box was torn open and the bottle inside had a broken seal, would you buy it? If you noticed its label was fraught with spelling errors, would you go ahead and ingest the medicine anyway? I'm guessing your answers are *no*.

This is because a product's credibility and safety impact someone's ability to use and benefit from that product. To have good over-the-counter data (OTCD) that is thus easy for educators to use—just as with good over-the-counter medicine—the package/display of the contents (e.g., data) must establish and maintain credibility.

A data system or report must have credibility to ensure its use. A credible data system or report suite is one users can trust as accurate, appropriate, and secure.

Fortunately, some of the hurdles that stood in the way of educators' technology use are dissolving with time. For example, teachers indicated overwhelming support for using technology to improve learning, and 85 percent of teachers reported daily use of technology to support teaching (Bill and Melinda Gates Foundation, 2012). Time also brings improvement in the value educators assign to data and its analysis. For example, most educators are now eager to analyze and then act on the data they see (Hattie, 2010; van der Meij, 2008). However, many still do not. For example, Underwood, Zapata-Rivera, and VanWinkle (2008) found teachers do not value some data included in data system reports.

Sometimes the following comments are heard coming from educators:

- "Why are we giving this test [or entering these scores into the system] when no one ever looks at the results?"
- "I don't need a test to tell me how my kids are doing. I can already *see* how my kids are doing."
- "The District [or State] just wants this data in the system so they can 'come after' us like Big Brother."
- "I'd use data if I had the time, but I just don't have the time. It's not worth it."

Sometimes complaints are justified, in which case educators' valid concerns should be remedied. For example, you cannot blame them for suspecting no one will look at inputted scores if no one ever does look at inputted scores. However, often such complaints are at least partly due to bias. Even if educators do value data, considering that most educators struggle with data analyses, many educators simply do not like to work with data.

Since many data system users do not value data and/or do not like using data, it is especially necessary for data systems to try to keep educators from becoming frustrated and giving up on using the data system and its reports altogether. Much of this can be remedied by fluid navigation and ease-of-use (discussed later in this chapter). However, data systems can also prevent educators from giving up on the system's use by establishing and maintaining credibility.

Edward Tufte (2011), a leading expert in data visualization and reporting not exclusive to education, said the most important task of someone presenting data is to establish and keep credibility. Credibility means the data can be trusted (its source, its accuracy, etc.).

If someone is *reluctantly* using a data system or *reluctantly* viewing a data system report, he or she could already be looking for a reason to stop using it. Losing credibility would immediately give such a person a reason to stop using the data system or its reports. Even someone who loves the data system and loves data analysis will not—and *should* not—continue to trust reports and data that come from a data system unable to maintain credibility.

Common killers of a data system's credibility are:

- **wrong** data (e.g., "163 percent of female students");
- **inappropriate** displays or calculations (e.g., a line graph implying growth for scores that change in makeup and meaning each year);
- **sloppiness** (e.g., cut-off text).

See *Example 1* in the "Report Before and After Examples" file to see these concepts illustrated. In addition, credibility is lost if the system is not designed to keep data private (allowing access only as appropriate) and secure.

If your DSRP could not spend five minutes cleaning up an accidental change in font size, spelling errors, or poor formatting that was overlooked, how can educators trust the accuracy of the data it displays? The truth is, they cannot.

Key Features

When educators view a data report, it should give them answers to their specific questions as quickly and easily as possible. See *Example 2* in the "Report Before and After Examples" file and consider how the features shown within the *After* version of the report excerpt help to immediately answer educators' questions in relation to the measure for which scores are reported. Notice how the following key features address common questions educators might have:

- The **summaries/averages** in the last two table rows help answer "Did the rest of the district perform any different? When and in which areas?"
- The **calculations** in the last two columns help answer "Are my students proficient? Which ones? When?"

Tools

- The **vital data** on the whole school's performance help answer "How did my students compare to the rest of the school? In which areas were we weaker vs. stronger?"
- The **graphs** at the bottom help answer "Did my students show growth? In which areas?"
- The **clear headers** in the top three rows help answer "What types of data am I viewing?"

The answers to the above questions would have been far more difficult (and in some cases, impossible) to garner if the same data were reported like the *Before* version of *Example 2*.

Difficulty in using and understanding the data displayed in the *Before* version of *Example 2* would arise since the display is missing the key features shown in the *After* version:

- **Summaries/averages** are displayed to provide context and allow for comparison.
- **Calculations** are displayed for the user, as any mental calculation poses some risk in accuracy.
- **Vital data** is included in the report.
- **Graphs** are used for key information and are used well (e.g., they are not three-dimensional, since two-dimensional graphs are less likely to distort the viewer's understanding of actual values).
- **Clear headers** provide added information and distinguish between data types.

See *Example 1*, *Example 2*, and *Example 3* in the "Report Before and After Examples" file to see these concepts illustrated.

Unfortunately, many reports fail to include these key features. The time one person (e.g., programmer) spends adding and/or improving key features within a report is minuscule compared to the time it will save all educators using the report. More importantly, the successful incorporation of key features will significantly reduce the chances of the report's data being misunderstood, misused, and/or not used at all.

Design

A large portion of educators are already intimidated by data. Many teachers and administrators do not know fundamental analysis concepts, and 70 percent have never taken a college or postgraduate course in educational measurement (Zwick et al., 2008). Only three states have implemented policies and practices ensuring educators know how to analyze and use data appropriately (National Association of States Boards of Education, 2012). For example, few teacher preparation programs cover topics like state data literacy (Halpin & Cauthen, 2011; Stiggins, 2002).

In fact, few educators are trained statisticians who automatically know how to use available data effectively (Data Quality Campaign, 2009), and most people responsible for analyzing data have received no training to do so (Few, 2008). This is even the case among administrators, even though principals rate the ability to use data as the most important skill needed to be a good principal (Metropolitan Life Insurance Company, 2013).

Fortunately, these challenges can be reduced by good design. Consider the role design can play in making data analysis easier and less intimidating:

- Teachers are far more likely to use data if it is presented in a user-friendly format (Rennie Center for Education Research and Policy, 2006).
- Reporting format impacts how useful data is to stakeholders (Hamilton & Koretz, 2002).
- Improving a data system's design and reporting can ease some of the growing pains that occur as teachers increase their use of a data system (Underwood et al., 2008).

There is a distinction between designing reports and designing reports in a way that assists analyses. Please see box overleaf.

Design recommendations for making data work could fill multiple books. For example, there are many great books by data visualization experts (e.g., Edward Tufte and Stephen Few) who specialize in the visual display of data not exclusive to education data, but whose findings can still be very helpful in determining good ways to display data for educators. Likewise, there is an abundance of web and interface design literature that can help inform the navigation design of a data system.

Tools

Experience from the Field

"After a K-12 school district's data team is completed with the myriad of accountability and compliance tasks and all the boxes of archaic paper and pencil tests are shrink-wrapped and sent to the State for scoring, my assessment and data analysis team can finally get around to our 'real' work. That is, supporting principals and teachers in the important task of providing clearly visualized data that impacts decisions regarding student performance. This is the work we do when the whirlwind is not overtaking our time; it is the work that got us into the business in the first place. Along the way we have encountered some formidable foes to graphical displays of complex information. The effects of these foes have rendered the landscape of meaningful data analysis littered with countless silly notebooks, indecipherable charts, pie graphs, and dead-end products that numb the minds of even the most ardent educators. The sad result is that well-meaning data/information becomes disconnected from critical decision-making and what is left to run the schools is assumptions and best guesses. My team has encountered these foes in the following categories:

1. **Fragmented data:** *Data is presented in a fragmented, multi-page format that prohibits comparisons. E.g., notebooks, packets, PDF docs.*
2. **Inadequate data:** Fails to answer users' questions.
3. **Inaccessible data:** Data is unavailable or spread over too many locations. E.g., SIS, data warehouses, third party programs.
4. **Indecipherable data:** Users don't know how to read the data as presented. E.g., pie graphs, spreadsheets.
5. **Stale data:** Data that is no longer relevant by the time of presentation.
6. **Useless data:** Data that is fraught with bias and peripheral noise and is not useful in driving future decision-making. E.g., most federal/state accountability data.

Package/Display

> Although these foes appear fatal, they are not. There is a better way. Teams that transform their data acquisition and data displays with disciplined and well researched, proven practices of data visualizations can and do overcome, but it takes a purposeful transformation and the grit to say 'NO' to bad past practice."
>
> —George Knights, Director of Professional Learning Communities and K-12 Assessment, Newport-Mesa Unified School District

However, some guidelines that are good for data displayed for people who are not education stakeholders sometimes require tweaking when it comes to education's unique data and its unique educator users. Other data display guidelines are somewhat subjective outside the realm of education, but when it comes to displaying data for education stakeholders in an effective way, the scales are tipped toward a clear winner.

Thus the OTCD Standards contained in this book focus on design decisions that are commonly poorly navigated by data system/report providers and/or are not as easily understood by existing design research that is not exclusive to education. OTCD *Design* Standards focus on avoiding common design mishaps to which education data systems and reports often fall victim, to the detriment of educators' data analyses. *Before* and *after* examples illustrate how each of these good design practices can be applied to education data reports:

- **The report's format** and components should be those most likely to encourage understanding and easy use of the data.
- **Avoid clutter** (e.g., use lines sparingly, include white space, etc.).
- **Avoid keys/legends**, as every time a graph asks a user to look away, find a key or legend, or gather knowledge on a color or character's meaning, and then look back at the chart again to apply that knowledge . . . it risks losing the user's understanding or attention.
- **Place the most important data in prime locations** (e.g., important "summary columns" should not be lost in the middle of a table when

Tools

these high-use columns can be more easily spotted at the end of the table).

- **Use proximity** within reports (e.g., juxtaposing multiple subgroups, years, measures, etc.) to encourage important comparisons.
- **Allow the user's eye to scan** across a report or section without encountering visual obstacles that impede common comparisons.
- **Center data** within cells in almost all cases rather than left-justifying figures (when numbers "hug" cell borders they are harder to distinguish).
- **Purposeful color and shading** help users navigate and understand content.
- **Use size** to reflect importance (e.g., if information is presented in a smaller font size, it should be because this information is deemed less important).
- **Do not over-complicate or over-simplify** a report's display; rather, use a simple-yet-effective design that will not overwhelm users, and avoid jargon.

See *Example 1* through *Example 3* in the "Report Before and After Examples" file to see these concepts illustrated.

Navigation

Within a data system or other computerized reporting environment, *navigation* is also often used to describe the buttons, links, menus, and other user interface tools that can be used to navigate through the system. Navigation tools are most likely to be seen and used when placed at the

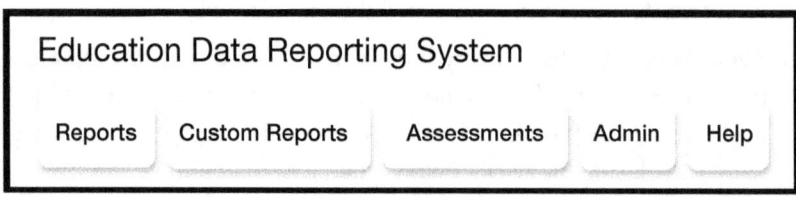

Figure 6.2 Sample Navigation Toolbar Seen on the Screen when Using a Data System

top of a webpage (Outing & Ruel, 2006). This means the buttons or links users click to access reports (to share, build, print, customize, etc.) in the data system are typically featured at the top of the webpage, often within a navigation bar (see, for example, Figure 6.2), though sometimes they appear on the side.

This bar of navigation options commonly remains ever-present, even when the user scrolls down the page (i.e., the navigation options remain "frozen" even when the rest of the page changes).

"Over-the-counter" (i.e., easy) navigation allows educators to use and move through a data system or other reporting environment with ease. This involves:

- how educators move through the system and find reports (involving good design and the use of filters);
- how educators move from one report to the next (involving reports being consolidated to support multiple inquiries and also involving design consistency).

Data systems should offer a centralized, intuitive, user-friendly interface (in regard to navigation, drill-down, data selection, and more) for accessing all reports (SAS Institute, 2013). *Intuitive* means most users can figure out where to find things and how to accomplish tasks within the system, simply due to the system's smart design and logical placement/workings. For example:

- **Items (buttons/links/etc.)** should be placed in logical locations, where the user would most likely expect to find them. This arrangement is not limited to only items within the same page, but also to how items are organized across multiple pages (e.g., like an outline, how one menu extends to submenus, how one link leads to other links or items, etc.).
- **Moving through the system** should be fast. This means the system should aim for few clicks (meaning times users click something with the mouse's cursor) without crowding the interface with too many clickable options. The interface must strike a balance between easy-to-navigate placement and the need to limit clicks.
- **The arrangement** should work for as many users as possible, so it should not be assumed that every user is tech-savvy. For example, the

tech-savvy programmers and developers who typically build a data system are not the only ones who need to find the system intuitive.

Educators are busy people, and any time a data system steals from them by being slow or difficult to use is time that is stolen from the students who educators want to use their time helping. Good navigation design that renders a system easy and fast to use is imperative.

One way in which data systems often fail to provide effective navigation is by failing to consolidate reports. For example, many data systems provide a long list of reports that are identical in most ways, with minor variations, and users must wade through this list to find the report they need.

Not only is this arrangement cumbersome to navigate, but it also requires longer processes to flip back and forth between reports during data investigation. Ideally, educators should be able to open a single report type and then use its input controls to select a particular test, group of students, test year, academic year, type of entity to list in the report, etc. Consolidated reports are vital, as they lend the user the power to shape the report to his or her specific needs.

Part of the reason this is ideal relates to clutter (e.g., too much information in report titles creates clutter, having too many reports on a list of report options creates clutter, etc.). However, a large part of why this is ideal relates to research on the best ways to approach data analysis.

Educators are sometimes trained in a specific approach to data investigation, such as the use of essential questions or data dialogues. Some approaches to analysis involve a combination of strategies, such as Bernhardt's (2004) popular recommendation to identify a problem, then hunches and hypotheses, and then questions before accessing data.

Each of these methods gets at the bigger questions and needs that are driving data investigation. For example, only an educator needing data in order to report it to another (such as for accountability) would simply want to know, "How did my students score on *that test*?" Typically, though an educator might seem driven by this question on the surface, a number or score has little meaning. What the educator really wants to know in this example, based on this test, is something along these lines:

- Did my students perform well?
- Did my students show improvement?

- How did my students perform in relation to my colleagues?
- How did my subgroups of students perform in relation to one another?
- When considered with multiple measures, did the new reading program I'm using likely help my students' performance? etc.

As 80 percent of teachers know, it is advisable to use multiple measures for data-informed decision-making (USDEOPEPD, 2011). For example, it is not advisable to focus on a single test when using data. Yet many report lists are comprised mainly of single-test reports (e.g., a test name is featured in the report title) and often lack reports on non-test data.

Thus most data systems' report titles do notoriously little to facilitate recommended data investigation practices. For example, consider how a single reporting investigation can be expressed in three data investigation methods/prompts:

- **Question:** Did I help raise my students' ability to analyze literature last year?
- **Theory:** I helped raise my students' ability to analyze literature last year.
- **Topic:** My students' growth—or lack of growth—in literature analysis last year.

The question, theory, and topic given above constitute a very common reason an educator would want to use a data system and its reports. However, compare that question, theory, and topic to an actual list of report titles in your data system. Is there a clear relationship between the two? The answer is often *no*. Rather, data system reports are often *test* focused.

The way most data reports are set up, with a different report title (and thus a different report on the report list) for each measure, educators have to go through the following steps whenever they view the results of one measure (e.g., Test A) and want to switch to another measure type (e.g., Portfolio A). Please see Figure 6.3 overleaf.

Often data inquiries are not linear, and educators must "flip back and forth" between in-depth results. This means leaving one data source's test's (or other measure's) results but then returning to them again to check something when other results trigger a notion. Thus the problem of reports being arranged by test rather than by data inquiry is compounded. If reports are also separated by format (e.g., *Run by Course*), the problem is further compounded.

Tools

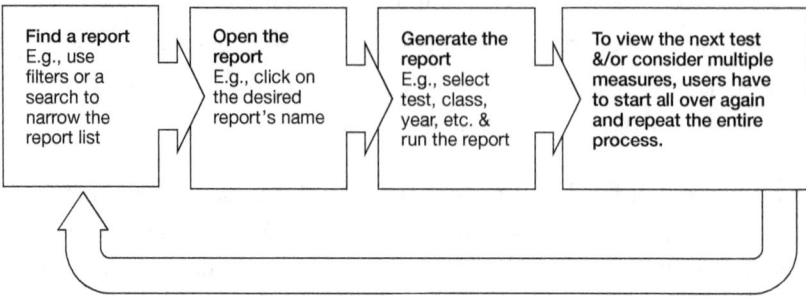

Figure 6.3

Now consider how the data investigation is improved by consolidating reports and letting users control a report's variations through its input controls (notice how the bottom arrow has moved). Please see Figure 6.4 below.

Other examples of how navigation impacts data investigation are shared in the "Package/Display" chapter in *Designing Data Reports that Work: A Guide for Creating Data Systems in Schools and Districts*. However, this section illustrates how good navigation needs to be planned with a thorough understanding of good design practice but also a thorough understanding of good *educator* practice.

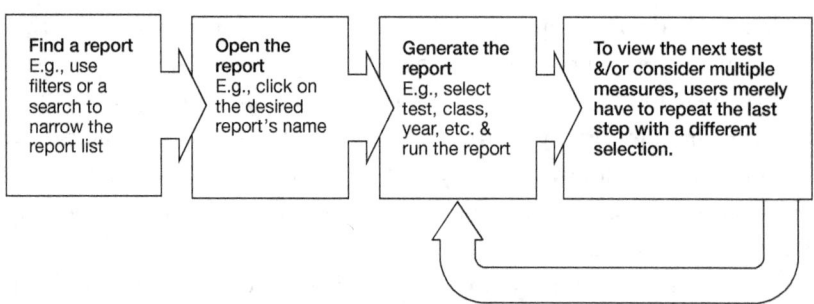

Figure 6.4

Input Controls

Input controls allow users to customize the manner in which a report is generated. This allows the same report to serve multiple functions, thus limiting the list of reports to a manageable size. In the upcoming example shown, the educator uses the *School* input control to select *N. D. Middle* from the drop-down menu so the *Subgroup Summary* report will display data only from N. D. Middle School. Please see Figure 6.5 overleaf.

> **Input controls** are the means through which a user communicates selected info to the data system (e.g., a drop-down menu of options).

Input controls should support good data investigation practices (covered in the previous section) and be organized for easy use. For example, imagine a grocery store where aisles were not devoted to specific purposes. Rather than seeing an aisle for snacks, another aisle for cleaning and paper goods, another aisle for bread and baked goods, and so on, you would have a difficult time finding and selecting the paper towels you ran into the store to buy if all product categories were jumbled together.

The same is true of input controls. Like filters used to make a data system's report list more manageable, categorizing input controls (e.g., by *Scope*, *Test*, and *Students*, as shown on the previous page) can help users run a report faster, more easily, and with more confidence.

Over-the-Counter Data Standards

An ideal data reporting environment should reflect the OTCD *Package/Display* Standards, which stipulate research-based ways data systems should display data. These standards can be found in the back of this book if you want to learn more about what qualifies as effective design.

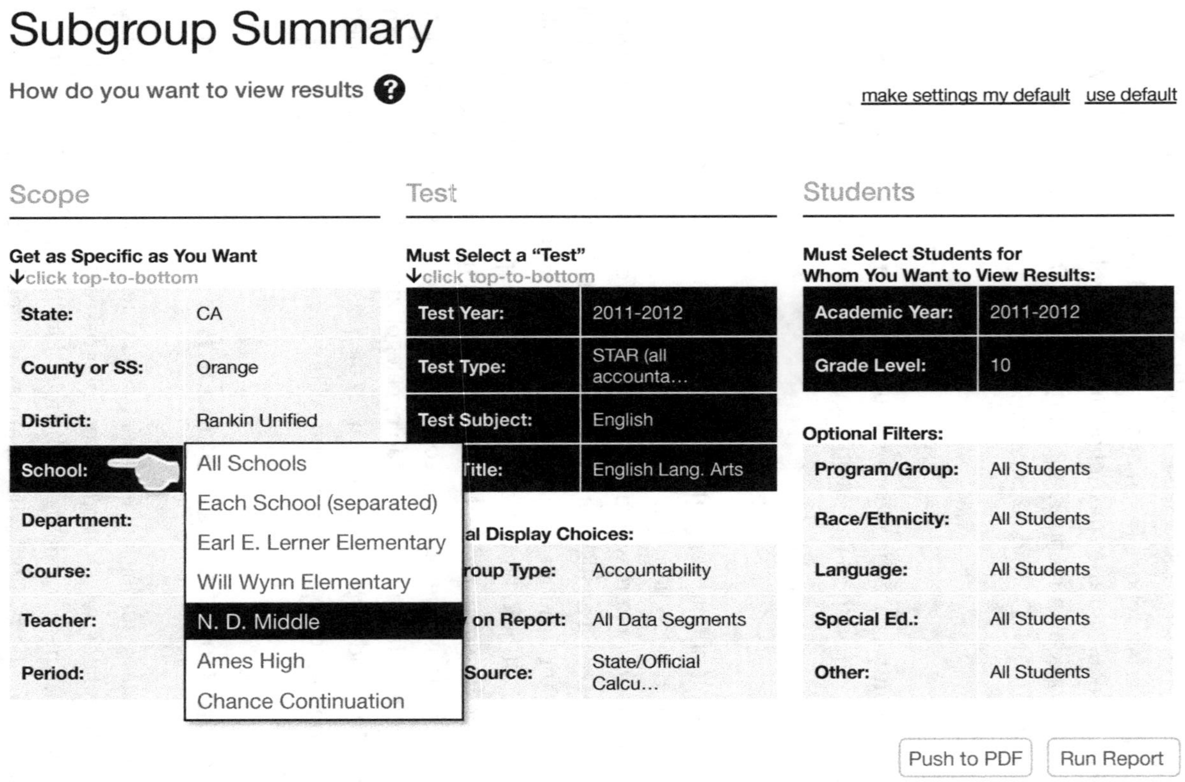

Subgroup Summary

How do you want to view results ❓

make settings my default   use default

Scope

Get as Specific as You Want
↓click top-to-bottom

State:	CA
County or SS:	Orange
District:	Rankin Unified
School:	All Schools
	Each School (separated)
	Earl E. Lerner Elementary
	Will Wynn Elementary
	N. D. Middle
	Ames High
	Chance Continuation
Department:	
Course:	
Teacher:	
Period:	

Test

Must Select a "Test"
↓click top-to-bottom

Test Year:	2011-2012
Test Type:	STAR (all accounta….
Test Subject:	English
Title:	English Lang. Arts

Additional Display Choices:

Group Type:	Accountability
on Report:	All Data Segments
Source:	State/Official Calcu….

Students

Must Select Students for Whom You Want to View Results:

Academic Year:	2011-2012
Grade Level:	10

Optional Filters:

Program/Group:	All Students
Race/Ethnicity:	All Students
Language:	All Students
Special Ed.:	All Students
Other:	All Students

[Push to PDF] [Run Report]

Figure 6.5

> **Good News**
>
> You are likely not the one who has to implement these standards. You only need to know they exist so you can ask for them. If you do want advanced support designing your own data reports, read *Designing Data Reports that Work: A Guide for Creating Data Systems in Schools and Districts*.

However, you are likely not the one who has to implement these standards. This book you are reading is for educator leaders, but there is a second book out there written for data system/report providers. Those who design, program, manage, and provide the data system/reports you use (as well as educators who design or build some of their own data reports) can read *Designing Data Reports that Work: A Guide for Creating Data Systems in Schools and Districts* by Dr. Jenny Grant Rankin for help with the process of implementing every OTCD *Package/Display* Standard.

Examples to Reference If Needed

Good design practices involve decisions of a visual nature. Thus many of the OTCD *Package/Display* Standards concepts that have been explained in this chapter can be better understood by looking at visual examples.

See the "Report Before and After Examples" file, where *before* and *after* report examples help illustrate how reports are rendered more effective when they package/display data better. The "Package/Display" chapter in *Designing Data Reports that Work: A Guide for Creating Data Systems in Schools and Districts* offers explanation of exactly how each of these examples was improved.

How to Get Effective Package/Display

You are likely not the one who has to implement effective package/display for your data system and its reports, which requires having the capacity to

Tools

manipulate the data system and its reports. If you do not have this ability (e.g., if a third party, such as a vendor, provides your data system/reports), the fastest and easiest way for you to get effective package/display is to advocate for it.

However, there are some aspects of data reports' credibility that are *only* within the school district's control. Thus there are some simple credibility steps you can implement or request of your colleagues.

If Someone Other Than You Provides Your Data System/Reports

The Best Approach: The best way for you to get a well-designed data system and reports is to ask for them. This book makes it easy for you to request effective package/display by providing an already-written email (shown on an upcoming page) you can send to your data system/report provider (DSRP). Simply copy/paste text from the electronic email into your own email, and modify/personalize your message as needed.

> ### Time-Saving Resource
> Copy/paste text from the following page's email into your own email.

Before you send the email:

1. Determine whether your data system and its reports are, indeed, designed poorly. Referencing the *Package/Display* standards in the back of this book can help you make this determination. Then you can enhance your email with details about specific problems you have noted.

2. Determine who at the DSRP is the best contact (this could be the Customer Service Department, but there is likely an implementation manager or other team member through whom you will find faster results).

3. Determine whether your district requires modification requests to go through a particular district administrator. In most cases it is appropriate for you to send the email yourself, but even then it is an advantage if district administrators *also* contact the DSRP advocating for effective design.
4. It is also recommended you read this book in its entirety so you can prioritize requests you send to your DSRP.

See the "Work With Your DSRP" chapter for details on how this initial step can initiate change in your data system/reports. That chapter will also guide you if any follow-up is necessary.

Email to DSRP for Package/Display

Dear Data System/Report Provider,

I noticed our district's data system and reports do not adhere to the Over-the-Counter Data *Package/Display* Standards that stipulate research-based ways to provide credibility, key features, and strong design within education data reports, as well as effective navigation and input controls. Adherence to these *Package/Display* standards is necessary to best support educators' easy use and thorough understanding of reports' data. Consider:

- A data system's report design, if done correctly, can free teachers from the need to be assessment-literate and instead allow them to focus on instruction and students (Hattie, 2010).
- Data reports designed for educators are frequently not designed in ways that are easy to interpret (VanWinkle, Vezzu, & Zapata-Rivera, 2011).
- Providing a data system designed specifically for users' needs is more effective than expecting training to get users as prepared as they need to be to use the system and its data (Underwood, Zapata-Rivera, & VanWinkle, 2008).

Tools

> Please attune our data system/reports to adhere to the research-based Over-the-Counter Data *Package/Display* Standards. These resources can help you:
>
> - Over-the-Counter Data Standards are available with other eResources (including details on the research behind each standard) at www.routledge.com/products/9781138956155 (the *Package/Display* standards are on pages 6–11).
> - Read the book *Designing Data Reports that Work: A Guide for Creating Data Systems in Schools and Districts,* by Dr. Jenny Grant Rankin. This guide explains how to implement each reporting standard within a data system/reports (offering specific examples, before and after illustrations, etc.).
>
> Thank you very much for your time and assistance. Adhering to these standards will offer tremendous help to educators and students.
>
> —Me
>
> Hattie, J. (2010). Visibly learning from reports: The validity of score reports. *Online Educational Research Journal.* Retrieved from www.oerj.org/View?action=viewPaper&paper=6
>
> Underwood, J. S., Zapata-Rivera, D., & VanWinkle, W. (2008) Growing pains: Teachers using and learning to use IDMSR. *ETS Research Memorandum. RM-08-07.* Princeton, NJ: ETS.
>
> VanWinkle, W., Vezzu, M., & Zapata-Rivera, D. (2011). Question-based reports for policymakers, *ETS Research Memorandum. RM-11-16.* Princeton, NJ: ETS.

However, sometimes problems with a data report's credibility (one aspect of good package/display) are due to problems with data the school district has provided. For example, district staff might have wrongly inputted data or provided the DSRP with poor data files. Steps you can implement or request of your colleagues to ensure cleaner, more accurate data include:

Package/Display

1. If you note suspicious data in your data system, alert your district office (e.g., the IT Department) and ask if an organized system is in place to double-check that original data files are as appropriately formatted, clean/correct, and complete as possible. For example, those involved in data input processes might utilize flowcharts to indicate who is responsible for each step in a dataset's journey into the data system (along with relevant resources and dates). These could vary widely by dataset. See Figure 6.6.

2. Ensure any staff responsible for inputting or managing data has access to a data input matrix to facilitate accuracy (see description ahead). This matrix should be uniform throughout the school district and thus come from the district office. You can determine if your district has such a matrix by asking for one.

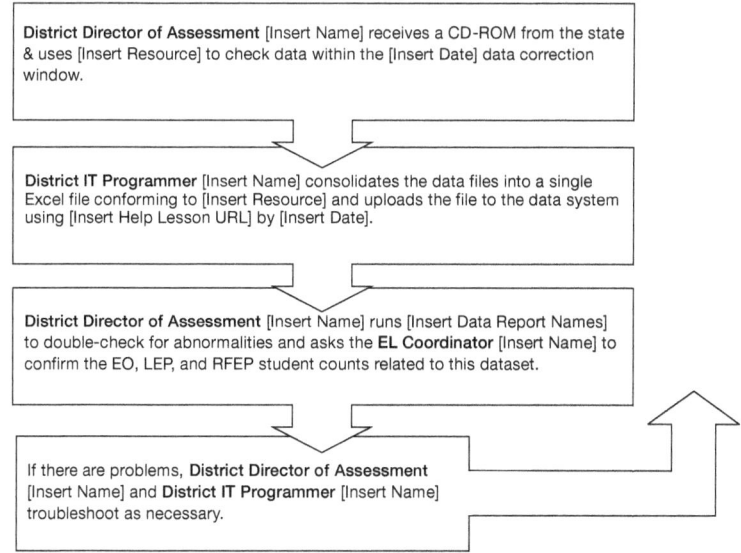

Figure 6.6 Example for State Language Proficiency Test A

Time-Saving Resource

Copy/paste text from the upcoming page's email into your own email.

Tools

This book makes it easy for you to request a data input matrix by providing an already-written email you can send to whoever controls data quality for your school district (e.g., IT Director). Simply copy/paste text from the electronic email into your own email, and modify/personalize your message as needed.

Data Input Matrix

A district-wide matrix should be available for every key screen or data type in the data system, and each row should contain a single field's information:

- **field** (label in the system for a single datum; e.g., STU.PED)
- **description** (e.g., parent education level: the highest level of education completed by either of the student's known parents)
- **appropriate codes** to enter (e.g., 0 = Less Than High School Completion, 1 = High School Completion, etc.)
- **source** (e.g., data comes from Student Registration Form).

The following details can be supplied for a single matrix (if it is the same for all fields listed); otherwise, these details should be indicated for each field:

- **screen** (the page within the data system where the field appears)
- **who enters/changes?** (the role or name of the person responsible for entering the field's datum and making any changes to it)
- **contact for support?** (e.g., District Office Help Desk, 999-9999 x999).

Email to DO for Data Matrix

Dear District Office Administrator Overseeing Data Quality,

As you know, data quality is paramount to effective data use. I have read of the benefits to data cleanliness when staff has access to a district-wide data input matrix to guide them in understanding (and correctly inputting/managing data for) data system fields. For example, front office staff can use such a matrix when fielding registration forms or entering demographic changes, and teachers can use such a matrix if using data system information to complete non-computerized testing answer documents that missed pre-ID.

Can you please send me such a matrix? I've added some details below in case they can be of help. According to what I read, a district-wide matrix should be available for every key screen or data type in the data system (i.e., those used by staff), and each row should contain a single field's information:

- **field** (label in the system for a single datum, e.g., STU.PED)
- **description** (e.g., parent ed. level: highest level of education completed by either of the student's known parents)
- **appropriate codes** to enter (e.g., 0 = Less Than High School Completion, 1 = High School Completion, etc.)
- **source** (e.g., Student Registration Form).

I also read the following details can be supplied for a single matrix (if it is the same for all fields listed) but should otherwise be indicated for each field:

- **screen** (page within data system where field appears)
- **who enters/changes?** (role/name of person responsible for entering or changing the field's datum)
- **contact for support?** (e.g., Help Desk at 1-800 . . .).

> Thank you very much for your time and assistance. I realize creating such a matrix will be an extensive endeavor if our data system provider doesn't provide one and/or if our district has not yet created one, but I'm sure such a matrix would be widely used and effective.
>
> —Me

Be sure your staff understands why and how to use the data input matrix. Use can vary by role, such as front office classified staff versus certificated teachers. Also, remind staff to use the matrix during possible data entry times, such as the start of the school year (e.g., office staff and counselors fielding new student registration) and testing (e.g., teachers completing non-computerized testing answer documents missing pre-ID).

The Less Desirable Approach: While educator leaders can control some aspects related to data reporting credibility, most package/display aspects are entirely within your DSRP's control. Ideally your DSRP will comply with the email you sent in the previous ("The Best Approach") section so you and your staff can benefit from effective package/display. However, depending on how many changes are needed, changing a data system's design can be a lengthy process and typically involves added programming time on the DSRP's end.

While your email might have initiated good practices, there is more you can do to encourage faster turnaround from your DSRP. This mostly involves offering details on specific changes that can be made. Here are some opportunities to help your DSRP fix two of the most harmful package/display problems:

- **If displayed data is wrong** (e.g., two reports give two widely different accounts of how many Students with Disabilities are in your district), you can help uncover the root cause of the problem. For example, since the DSRP is far removed from the students, the DSRP will not likely know at a glance that a number is clearly "off" in the way an educator often will.

Work with key stakeholders familiar with the students represented by the data (e.g., district administrators and site office staff) to get an idea for what the data *should* look like (e.g., How many GATE students do we have? How many students in the SDC classes do we have? etc.). Determine:
- what data is wrong (e.g., all reports showing our number of RFEP students—Reports A, B, and C—look right for all years except 2014, for which an incorrect RFEP number is displayed);
- how you know it's wrong (e.g., our EL Dept. confirmed there is no way 90 percent of our students are RFEP); and
- what a more accurate account would look like (for the last 3 years our SARC says 5.1–6.2 percent of our students are RFEP, and we have not made any major changes to our redesignation practices).

If possible, troubleshoot whether or not the issue lies in file(s) you inputted or provided to the DSRP. Save any relevant screenshots and/or generated reports and share all details with your DSRP. These specific details will likely render a speedier fix.

Based on what is determined to be the problem and how the system's data tables are structured, you can also double-check any other reports that might have a similar problem to the one that was found. In some cases (but not all), fixing the data problem for one report also solves it for other reports.

- **If a display or calculation is inappropriate** (e.g., 2014's accountability score is subtracted from 2015's accountability score and the difference is graphed as "growth" even though the scores differ in meaning year-to-year), your DSRP can benefit from learning why such a design is wrong. This problem often occurs when the same data report format is used for different measures (e.g., State A's Graduation Assessment versus State B's Graduation Assessment) without the DSRP understanding the measures' different limitations.

Let your DSRP know:
- the specific problem (e.g., where the flawed display or calculation appears, as circled in a fully generated report in which the problem is visible);
- what would be an appropriate fix (e.g., how the calculation should be made, the scores graphed, the difference described, etc.); and

- what proof there is that the change should be made (such as a link and page number for the explanatory paragraph in the post-test guide authored to accompany a particular assessment).

To help you spot problems, examples of mistakes that data systems and reports commonly make are featured ahead. Please see Table 6.1 on page 98.

If You Provide Your Own Data System/Reports

If you provide your own data system/and or reports, you are in luck. You have direct control over the design of your staff's reporting environment. This section can also help if you provide just some of your own reports, such as building custom reports to supplement those that your data system offers prebuilt.

The following steps and tools will help you ensure your data system and reports are designed effectively:

1. Determine what (if any) problems exist in your reporting environment in regard to credibility, key features, design, navigation, and input controls. Referencing the *Package/Display* standards in the back of this book can help.

2. Consult with key stakeholders at your district before working on design changes. For example, an administrators' meeting might reveal teachers are overly confused by how to use the data system, in which case revamping navigation might take top priority. It is also recommended you read this book in its entirety so you can prioritize changes.

3. Reference the "Package/Display" chapter in *Designing Data Reports that Work: A Guide for Creating Data Systems in Schools and Districts*. The lessons in this chapter explain how to best implement each *Package/Display* standard (offering specific examples, before and after illustrations, etc.). If you want a summary of research behind each *Package/Display* standard, read the research information available.

4. Using the resources in the box below, implement report and data system design that conforms to specific OTCD Standards.

Plenty of Help

Your DSRP (or anyone else designing reports and/or a data system) can use:

- "Package/Display" chapter in *Designing Data Reports that Work: A Guide for Creating Data Systems in Schools and Districts* (containing a lesson for implementing each OTCD)

References

Bernhardt, V. L. (2004). *Data analysis for continuous school improvement.* Larchmont, NY: Eye on Education.

Bill and Melinda Gates Foundation. (2012). *Innovation in education: Technology and effective teaching in the U.S.* Retrieved from www.edsurge.s3.amazonaws.com/public/BMGF_Innovation_In_Education.pdf

Data Quality Campaign. (2009). *The next step: Using longitudinal data systems to improve student success.* Retrieved from www.dataqualitycampaign.org/find-resources/the-next-step/

Few, S. (2008, November 14). Telling compelling stories with numbers: Data visualization for enlightening communication. Statewide Longitudinal Data Systems (SLDS) Grant Program Third Annual Fall Grantee Meeting. Presentation conducted from SLDS, Arlington, VA. Retrieved from www.nces.ed.gov/programs/slds/pdf/08_F_06.pdf

Halpin, J., & Cauthen, L. (2011, July 31). The education dashboard. *Center for Digital Education's Converge Special Report 2*(3), 2–36.

Hamilton, L. S., & Koretz, D. M. (2002). Tests and their use in test-based accountability systems. In L. S. Hamilton, B. M. Stecher, & S. P. Klein (Eds.), *Making sense of test-based accountability in education*, 13–49. Santa Monica, CA: Rand.

Hattie, J. (2010). Visibly learning from reports: The validity of score reports. *Online Educational Research Journal.* Retrieved from www.oerj.org/View?action=viewPaper&paper=6

Metropolitan Life Insurance Company. (2013). *MetLife survey of the American teacher: Challenges for school leadership.* New York, NY: Author and Peanuts Worldwide.

National Association of States Boards of Education. (2012, December). *Born in another time: Ensuring educational technology meets the needs of students today—and tomorrow.* Arlington, VA: Author.

Outing, S., & Ruel, L. (2006, January 30). The Best of Eyetrack III: What we saw when we looked through their eyes. *Eyetrack III, 1–9. The Poynter Institute.* Retrieved from www.academia.edu/546755/The_best_of_eyetrack_III_What_we_saw_when_we_looked_through_their_eyes

Rennie Center for Education Research and Policy. (2006, February). *Data-driven teaching: Tools and trends.* Cambridge, MA: Rennie Center for Education Research and Policy.

SAS Institute. (2013). *Best practices in information management, reporting and analytics for education.* Retrieved from www.fs24.formsite.com/edweek/form15/secure_index.html

Stiggins, R. (2002). Assessment for learning. *Education Week, 21*(26), 30, 32–33.

Tufte, E. (2011, December 8) *Presenting Data and Information.* Presentation conducted from the Westin San Francisco Market Street, San Francisco, CA.

Underwood, J. S., Zapata-Rivera, D., & VanWinkle, W. (2008) Growing pains: Teachers using and learning to use IDMS®. *ETS Research Memorandum. RM-08–07.* Princeton, NJ: ETS.

U.S. Department of Education Office of Planning, Evaluation and Policy Development. (2011). *Teachers' ability to use data to inform instruction: Challenges and supports.* United States Department of Education (ERIC Document Reproduction Service No. ED516494).

Van der Meij, H. (2008). Designing for user cognition and affect in a manual. Should there be special support for the latter? *Learning & Instruction, 18*(1), 18–29.

VanWinkle, W., Vezzu, M., & Zapata-Rivera, D. (2011). Question-based reports for policymakers. E*TS Research Memorandum. RM-11–16.* Princeton, NJ: ETS.

Zwick, R., Sklar, J., Wakefield, G., Hamilton, C., Norman, A., & Folsom, D. (2008). Instructional tools in educational measurement and statistics (ITEMS) for school personnel: Evaluation of three web-based training modules. *Educational Measurement: Issues and Practice, 27*, 14–27.

Table 6.1 Common Data Displays and Calculations that Can Be Inappropriate

Analysis	If This Is True of Your Data:	...Then It Is Inappropriate to Use This Calculation/Display:	...and Inappropriate to Encourage a Conclusion Like This Example:
Accountability Growth	Accountability criteria differ over the years (e.g., with changes to benchmarks/requirements, assessments, weights, etc.)	Juxtaposing yes/no status over time as if each year's status means the same thing or subtracting one year's accountability growth score (rather than base score offered for comparison, or tracking degree of growth) from the next year's growth score and so on to determine growth, or using a display that encourages such a comparison	"Our school made Adequate Yearly Progress (AYP) 2008–2010, but not 2011–2014, so our students are dropping in performance."—or—"Our district's Growth Academic Performance Index (API) score was 680 in 2012, 690 in 2013, and 700 in 2014, so our district's students showed improvement."
Grade-to-Grade Comparisons	The assessments are not vertically scaled, meaning their difficulty differs (in relation to students tested) from one year to the next.	Subtracting the average score of students in one grade level from the average score of students in another grade level on tests from a series (e.g., state Math tests) to determine how much one grade "beat" the other, or	"352 was the average score of Grade 7 students at my school on the 2014 Grade 7 State Math Test, whereas 368 was the average score of Grade 6 students at our feeder school on the 2014 Grade 6 State Math

		a display that encourages such a comparison	Test, so our school's students performed more poorly than our feeder's students."
Year-to-Year Comparisons	**The assessments are scaled from one year to the next so the same test's difficulty is maintained (in relation to students tested) from one year to the next.**	Subtracting the average raw score (rather than scale score) of students from one year (e.g., 2013) from the average raw score of students the next year (e.g., 2014) on the same test (e.g., Test A) to determine which year performed better, or using a display that encourages such a comparison	"My 2014 10th graders had a 345 average raw score on the 2014 Grade 10 State English Test, whereas my 2013 10th graders had a 321 average raw score on the 2013 Grade 10 State English Test. I must have improved my teaching skills."
Cohort Growth	**The assessments are not vertically scaled, meaning their difficulty differs (in relation to students tested) from one year to the next.**	Subtracting a cohort's (the same group of students') scores from one year (e.g., 2013) from their scores the next year (e.g., 2014) on tests from a series (e.g., state Math tests) to determine growth, or using a display that encourages such a comparison	"My Grade 3 students' average score was 382 on the 2014 State Math Test when they were in Grade 3 (with me), and these same students averaged 373 on the 2013 State Math Test when they were in Grade 2 (with other teachers), so my students' performance improved."

Table 6.1 Continued

Analysis	If This Is True of Your Data:	...Then It Is Inappropriate to Use This Calculation/Display:	... and Inappropriate to Encourage a Conclusion Like This Example:
Domain-to-Domain Comparisons	**The assessment's domains (i.e., questions aligned to them) differ in difficulty, meaning some domains are harder than others**	Comparing performance in one domain of the test to performance in another domain/cluster/area of the same test as if the domains of the test are equally difficult, or using a display that encourages such a comparison	"My Grade 7 students averaged 76% correct in the *Reading Comprehension* cluster (on Test A in 2013), and the same group of students averaged 65% correct in the 2013 *Writing Strategies* domain (on Test A in 2013), so I did a better job teaching *Reading Comprehension* than I did teaching *Writing Strategies*."
Year-to-Year Domain Growth	**The same domain (i.e., questions aligned to it) varies in difficulty from one year to the next, meaning it can get harder or easier for students taking the test**	Subtracting students' average score for a particular domain one year from students' average score for a particular domain the next year to determine how much instruction for the	"My students averaged 74% correct in the *Reading Comprehension* cluster in 2013, and then they averaged 74% correct in the *Reading Comprehension* cluster in 2014,

		domain at that grade level improved, or using a display that encourages such a comparison	so my students' scores did not improve. I need to improve in teaching Reading Comprehension."
Cohort Domain Growth	**The same domain (i.e., questions aligned to it) varies in difficulty (in relation to students tested) from one grade level to the next, meaning it can get harder or easier for students taking the test** -or- **Domains are not vertically scaled (i.e., their difficulty doesn't grow in equal increments) from one grade level to the next, even if the tests are.**	Subtracting students' average score for a particular domain one year from the same group of students' average score for the same domain the next year (i.e., in the next grade level) to determine growth, or using a display that encourages such a comparison	"My Grade 7 students averaged 76% correct in the *Reading Comprehension* cluster in 2013, and they averaged 67% correct in the *Reading Comprehension* cluster when they were in Grade 6, so these students grew by 9 percentage points. I have bettered their *Reading Comprehension* skills."

7 Content

What Is Content?

If an over-the-counter pill marketed as a cold remedy really contained nothing but sugar and food coloring, it would not help cure your cold. A product is useless—no matter how well you package it or embed support for its use—if a product's content does not do what users need it to do. The ingredients of the product are vital.

For example, if someone buys a product to stop a fever, the product should stop a fever. It's OK for a product to have multiple uses, but these uses are usually specific and not overly numerous. Also, expired medications are removed from shelves so as not to poison users. Thus over-the-counter product content remains effective.

The same is true of data reports and data systems. Great labeling, supplemental documentation, help system support, and an effective package/display will be useless in helping educators and their students if the data system reporting *content* does not do what educators need it to do.

Data system reporting content consists of:

- what you get within each report once the reports are opened
- the report offering as a whole (i.e., the suite of reports)

To be "over-the-counter" and thus easy to use, each report's content should be appropriate for intended audiences, and "expiration" should be considered (e.g., calculations and textual guidance such as footers should be kept current with changing legislation and user needs). Likewise, the *suite* of reports should be a streamlined collection that covers all key needs without overwhelming users.

Why and How Should Data Reports Contain Effective Content?

Should medicine that expired in 1997 still be sitting on a drugstore shelf, ready for sale? No—that would be dangerous for consumers. The same is true of data system and report contents that are out-of-date. If these outdated contents are used to treat the needs of students, they can lead to flawed conclusions and flawed data-informed decisions, which can hurt students. Please see Table 7.1 overleaf.

Each Report

Reports should reflect the latest legislation, common user needs, research, and technology. A report's content should also be designed around its predetermined audience. Even when users are all educators, these users can still vary widely in terms of knowledge, skills, role, region, and needs. These audience differences can warrant special consideration for report aspects such as:

- terms used
- terms defined
- explanations provided
- components excluded versus included
- report format to accommodate region-specific assessment's reporting requirements.

For example, a report designed for a student should be less complicated and use simpler language than a report designed for a teacher or administrator.

Table 7.1 Changes with which Reports and Report Suites Must Remain Current

Change Type	Change Examples
Legislation	• Accountability (requirements, components, etc.) • Tests (those used, the way they are reported, levels tested, etc.) • Criteria (graduation, retention, status, redesignation, etc.) • Demographics (name, definition, qualifying criteria, etc.) • Calculations (data included, subject weights, etc.)
User Needs	• Speed with which data is needed • Growing term familiarity • Popular classroom technology
Research	• New approaches to data use • Extensive (as opposed to no or minimal) predictive analytics. For example, consider: when students at Purdue University took at least two courses that used the university's data mining and analysis software, which provided both teachers and students with data-informed feedback on risk of poor student performance, graduation rates were 21.48% higher (Tally, 2013).
Technology	• Integrating reports with results- and audience-based professional learning models, curriculum, and other tools specifically designed to remedy any problems indicated by the data. E.g., a 184,000-student school district in Fairfax County, Virginia hopes to enhance its curriculum and assessment resource system to make data-informed intervention recommendations to teachers (Davis, 2013). • Allowing a question- or theory-based search to render a report generated in a way that specifically addresses the question or theory that was posed. • Providing an expressed question with its exact answer(s). This is similar to the above notion, but the answer would be explicitly stated for the user.

Report Suite

A good reporting environment is one that does not surrender to complacency, but rather constantly reflects a "we can always get better" mindset of the team behind it. In addition to improvements necessitated by changing times, the report suite should also reflect a proactive design approach organized to cover all key needs without overwhelming users. In other words, you do not want too many reports to navigate, but you also do not want there to be gaps between what is reported versus what educators *need* to have reported.

Reporting gaps occur when one or both of the following occur:

- Key, needed data analyses are not facilitated by any reports in the report suite.
- Key, needed data analyses can only be accommodated when reports and/or features not intended for those analyses have to be used (e.g., in a cumbersome way) because no better alternatives exist in the report suite.

One of the best ways to avoid reporting gaps is to build reports according to a pre-drafted needs matrix. A needs matrix is a document that details educators' key data reporting needs that need to be covered by the report suite. An example of a needs matrix is provided on upcoming pages, followed by an explanation of its components. Later in this chapter you will learn how to download a template of this matrix, which you can adapt to suit your own school district's needs. Unfortunately, many DSRPs are designing, building, and deploying reports one-by-one in a reactive model driven by client/educator requests. While it is vital to listen to clients/educators and respond to their needs, a reactive approach to report building is ill equipped to improve educators' data analysis problems.

Tools

NEEDS MATRIX	REPORT TOPIC & SAMPLE INVESTIGATIONS SUPPORTED		FORMAT		
	Report Topic (Can Be Modified for Title, Possibly with Format Added) & Sample Data Investigations Report Type Can Be Used to Address: - Sample Question Formula - Sample Question - Sample Theory		Entities	Measures/Datasets	Years/Times
Correlation (Includes Predictive)	**1-to-1 Correlation** How does/did _ affect or correlate with _? How do student grades correlate with standardized assessment performance? Mobility decreases students' sense of belonging at our school.		Single	Multiple	Single
	1-to-1 Correlation Change How (and to what extent) will/did changing _ impact _? Will improving stud. reading skills positively affect their perform. in core courses & state+local assessments? Participation in after-school intervention will improve graduation status.		Single	Multiple	Multiple
	Correlation Identification What other characteristics do _ share? What characteristics do graduating students share? Teachers who leave the district within 3 years are mostly 1st-time teachers.		Single	Multiple	Varies
	Correlation Change Indentification What has been associated with improved _? What can our school do to improve student discipline? Implementing a stronger discipline policy & Sat. School correlated with reduced staff attrition in our school.		Single	Multiple	Multiple
Focus	**Entity's Measure Focus** How did _ perform on the _ measurement tool? How many GATE students are enrolled in school this year? On the mid-year survey, parents indicated low confidence in school safety.		Single	Single	Single
	Entity's Area Focus How did _ perform in the area of _? How did our 4th grade group perform in writing on all of this year's measures? My RSP students are entering my classroom without higher-order thinking skills.		Single	Multiple	Single
Breakdown	**Entity's Measure Breakdown** How did _ respond to each _ on the _ tool/assessment/survey/etc.? How did my class respond to each question on the End of Year Survey? Alotta struggled more with Qs at the end of the test than the beginning.		Single	Single	Single

Figure 7.1

Content

Breakdown	**Multiple Entities' Measure Breakdown** How did each _ respond to each _ on the _ tool/assessment/survey/etc.? How did my 8th grade class periods answer high Bloom's level Qs on last yr.'s BM4 test? As I debrief the exam's Qs with my class, each seating group will have at least 1 stud. who answered Q right.	Multiple	Single	Single
Overview	**Entity's Multiple Measure Overview** How did _ perform on these many measurement tools: _? Did Khan struggle more on the portfolio assessments than on the tests? The intervention program is going strong when it comes to assignments.	Single	Multiple	Varies
	Entity's Multiple Area Overview How did _ perform in these many areas: _? Is my child ready to apply for (and get into) a UC-level college? When I look at the dashboard I will see our school's 7th grade class is strongest in all core subjects.	Single	Multiple	Varies
Comparison (Includes Ranking & Gaps)	**Multiple Entities' Measure Comparison** How did each _ perform on the _ measurement tool? How do students' reading skills vary within each of my class periods? Some socio-ec. levels have a higher proportion of students below grade level on the LP exam than others.	Multiple	Single	Single
	Multiple Entities' Area Comparison How did each _ perform in the area of _? How do our schools compare in writing, according to our district's various writing measures? Our lower grades are stronger in reading than the higher grades.	Multiple	Multiple	Single
Comparison (Continued)	**Multiple Entities' Multiple Measure Comparison** How did each _ perform on these many measurement tools: _? What are my son's final exam scores in each class? Some subgroups have a higher proportion of students performing below grade level in ELA than others.	Multiple	Multiple	Varies
	Multiple Entities' Multiple Area Comparison How did each _ perform in these many areas: _? What does my class roster look like and what are each student's general needs? I have at least 5 EL students in 3rd period, and they all have low scores in ELA.	Multiple	Multiple	Varies
Criteria (Includes Predictive)	**Fit Criteria Identification** What _ fit the criteria of _? Which students are at risk of dropping out? There are at least 35 students on the Honor Roll.	Varies	Varies	Single
	Requirement Fulfillment What are the answers/data for specific Qs/requests coming from _? What can I turn in as my SARC? My ELSSA Report will look like...	Single	Multiple	Multiple

Figure 7.1 Continued

Tools

Change (Including Growth, Can Be Cohort or Year-to-Year)	**Entity's Measure Change** How did _ change over the course of _ years/times on the _ measurement tool? How many retained kids went up a level on the state Math test? Trig's math students grew more in Number Sense than other domains on the district final.	Single	Single	Multiple
	Entity's Area Change How did _ change over the course of _ years/times in the area of _? How did high-referral students improve in perception of school? The Science Dept. had growth in hypothesis-crafting between Quarters 1 & 3.	Single	Varies	Multiple
	Entity's Multiple Measure Change How did _ change over the course of _ years/times on these many measurement tools: _? How did 1st year teachers at Will Wynn Elem. School change in their survey feedback by year end? The sites reached more of their SMART Goals this year than they did last year.	Single	Multiple	Multiple
	Entity's Multiple Area Change How did _ change over the course of _ years/times in these many areas: _? Did students noted as at-risk improve in college/career readiness? The site improved in most areas of the Health Kids Survey.	Single	Varies	Multiple
	Multiple Entities' Measure Change How did each _ change over the course of _ years/times on the _ measurement tool? How have last year's intervention students improved in reading? More Hispanic students than Asian students improved in word analysis.	Multiple	Single	Multiple
	Multiple Entities' Area Change How did each _ change over the course of _ years/times in the area of _? How many lowest-performing stud. on last yr.'s vocab exams improved in word analysis this yr.? Grade 7 made more progress in number sense than other grades did.	Multiple	Varies	Multiple
	Multiple Entities' Multiple Measure Change How did each _ change over the course of _ years/times on these many measurement tools: _? How did each department improve its integration of varied technologies? Each of my class period's students improved in word analysis.	Multiple	Multiple	Multiple
Position	**Position on Continuum** What is _'s position in the numerous ranked areas of the _ standards/rubric/scales? At which grade level is Paige performing on each of the CCSS ELA standards? Skip scored lower on the writing rubric categories related to style and voice than he did on mechanics.	Single	Single	Multiple

Figure 7.1 Continued

Aspects of the Needs Matrix

(Explaining Example on Previous Pages)

Terms Used in Matrix

Entities See bulleted examples in the *Entity* section, below.

Measures/Datasets A single measure or dataset means one test's scores, one evaluation's marks, one survey's responses, one demographics set, etc.; multiple measures/datasets would mean data from multiple sources, such as multiple tests' scores, multiple evaluations' marks, etc.

Years/Times This relates to the number of years' (or time periods, such as quarters) data is displayed for each measure/dataset and does not relate to the academic/enrollment year (which may be the same as or different from the measure/dataset year).

Topics Absorbed by Reports

Criterion-Based Growth Allow users to easily set criteria-based groups (e.g., run a fit list report or other means of generating a list of students, then save those students as a group like "students with 10+ truancies and 5+ detentions"), then have the ability to select the group with reports' input controls to generate reports with this group as the selected entity. Thus this topic does not require additional reports, as it can be absorbed by other reports.

Cohort vs. Year-to-Year Growth Allow users to select different year combinations (e.g., enrollment year vs. testing year) in order to report on a cohort *or* non-cohort basis.

When Running Each of These Reports

Entity Though not charted, when running any of the reports listed in the needs matrix, the user should have the ability to opt (through input control) to generate the report for one (and ideally each) of these entity levels:

Tools

- Student
- Program/Group
- Class Period
- Course
- Department
- Teacher
- Grade Level
- School
- District
- Similar School
- County
- State

Combos The ability to select combinations of entities or criteria is also helpful. For example, you might want to select a *Teacher* and *Grade Level* (e.g., to only show the results of teacher Anita Book's 7th grade students).

Audience and Format Though not charted, when running any of the reports listed in the needs matrix, the user should have the ability to generate the report topic for one (and nearly each) of these formats, which each have a version geared toward one audience (or a combination, as is sometimes appropriate for parent/student):

Format	Educator	Parent	Student	(Same Version for Parent/Student)
- List	X			
- Snapshot	X	X	X	X
- Description	X			
- Seating	X			
- Rubric	X	X	X	
- Grouping	X		X	
- Schedule	X	X	X	X
- Calendar	X	X	X	X
- Letter	X	X	X	
- Slip	X		X	

It is usually appropriate for the format to form the last word of the report's title. It is also appropriate for some formats to end with a snapshot.

Format Descriptions

List Each entity is listed in a row with data

Snapshot Often one page, a collection of graphs gives a summary/overview.

Description Heavy text is accommodated, such as lengthy survey Q&A.

Seating Results are displayed in a way that matches the class seating chart.

Rubric Results are shown within the context of a rubric's levels and criteria.

Grouping A teacher can see suggested groupings for differentiation, and a student can see all of his or her groups for various standards or activities.

Schedule The most common example is the class schedule.

Calendar Calendar format can juxtapose data (such as performance data) with information like a curriculum pacing guide, attendance, work completion, etc.

Letter A letter combines user-friendly explanation with data.

Slip Multiple slips print per page, allowing teachers to efficiently cut/hand out data that is specific to each student (e.g., each student's own test results print).

Imagine building a report suite as akin to building a house. A report suite must accommodate all of a user's key needs in a way that is easy to live with, just as a comfortable home must do this for its residents. Think of a DSRP that builds reports in a reactive manner as akin to a house builder who draws up architectural plans and then builds a single room for a house, then draws up plans and builds the next room, etc., without drawing up plans ahead of time for the entire house.

> ### *Needs Matrix*
>
> A *needs matrix* organizes educators' data analysis needs into types, around which report designs can be constructed in order to maximize report efficiency and offer reports in a streamlined, user-friendly manner.

Conversely, imagine the benefits of a DSRP that designs most of its suite of reports ahead of time. This is like a house builder who draws up architectural plans for the entire house ahead of time, then makes educated adjustments to the house plans only if necessary as each room is built.

There is a reason most houses are built from architectural plans in which the entire house has been designed. Sure, the homeowner might want to make an addition down the line or remodel a room in the future, but building the house from complete plans would render such changes more minimal. Having a plan ahead of time results in a better planned house, rooms that work well together to meet all of the resident's needs, the reduction of unnecessary repetition (e.g., three kitchens that work in slightly different ways but none of which meets all of the homeowner's needs), etc.

The same is true of data reporting environments and the need to plan the core report suite ahead of time. By using a needs matrix, a DSRP can avoid reporting gaps and unnecessary redundancy. Reporting redundancy occurs when many reports serve relatively the same purpose, only with slight variations. In some cases this requires users to run each of a series of reports to achieve a purpose when it would have been more efficient to run one report with all needed data. Redundancy contributes to clutter in a report suite, which makes the suite harder and more time-intensive to navigate.

Experience from the Field

"In Bonita USD, reading data is a priority for our elementary schools. We are currently reconsidering the correct content for our data report suites using multiple measures. The changes in accountability in recent years, and with Common Core State Standards, have given us the opportunity to reevaluate how we measure proficiency and success within our district. At the student level it is about how well the individual is progressing over time.

The story provided by the data gets more complicated as we look at program and how grade levels are progressing. We are working elbow to elbow with our principals to dig into what are the most important pieces of the student's story. These are lively discussions as we search for consensus to ensure each metric is meaningful. There is a steady balance between the stability of a measurement from year to year and the malleability of the data as accountability changes.

To continue to look at the data in the same way can become stale and irrelevant. Our district has benefited from having data tools that allow on-demand flexibility to tell the necessary story. Our next step is scaling that story for each view: a single student, a class, a grade level, a school, and finally the District as a whole."

—Kris Boneman, Director of Educational Technology
Bonita Unified School District

Over-the-Counter Data Standards

An ideal data reporting environment should reflect the OTCD *Content* Standards, which stipulate research-based ways data systems/reports can provide appropriate data report content. These standards can be found in the back of this book if you want to learn more about what qualifies as effective content.

Tools

> **Good News**
>
> You are likely not the one who has to implement these standards. You only need to know they exist so you can ask for them. If you do want advanced support creating your own data reports, read *Designing Data Reports that Work: A Guide for Creating Data Systems in Schools and Districts*.

However, you are likely not the one who has to implement these standards. This book you are reading is for educator leaders, but there is a second book out there written for data system/report providers. Those who design, program, manage, and provide the data system/reports you use (as well as educators who design or build some of their own data reports) can read *Designing Data Reports that Work: A Guide for Creating Data Systems in Schools and Districts* by Dr. Jenny Grant Rankin for help with the process of implementing every OTCD *Content* Standard.

How to Get Effective Content

You are likely not the one who has to implement effective content for your data system, which requires having the capacity to manipulate the data system and its reports. If you do not have this ability (e.g., if a third party, such as a vendor, provides your data system/reports), the fastest and easiest way for you to get effective content is to advocate for it.

If Someone Other Than You Provides Your Data System/Reports

The Best Approach: The best way for you to get effective data report content is to ask for it. This book makes it easy for you to request effective content by providing an already-written email (shown on page 116) you can send to your data system/report provider (DSRP). Simply copy/paste text from the electronic email into your own email, and modify/personalize your message as needed.

Time-Saving Resource

Copy/paste text from the following page's email into your own email.

Before you send the email:

1. Determine whether your data system does, indeed, contain poor content. Referencing the *Content* standards in the back of this book can help you make this determination. Then you can enhance your email with details about specific problems you have noted.
2. Determine who at the DSRP is the best contact (this could be the Customer Service Department, but there is likely an implementation manager or other team member through whom you will find faster results).
3. Determine whether your district requires modification requests to go through a particular district administrator. In most cases it is appropriate for you to send the email yourself, but even then it is an advantage if district administrators *also* contact the DSRP advocating for effective content.
4. It is also recommended you read this book in its entirety so you can prioritize requests you send to your DSRP.

See the "Work With Your DSRP" chapter for details on how this initial step can initiate change in your data system/reports. That chapter will also guide you if any follow-up is necessary.

The Less Desirable Approach: Ideally your DSRP will comply with the email you sent in the previous ("The Best Approach") section so you and your staff can benefit from optimal content. This book's "Work With Your DSRP" chapter will cover why you might look for a new data system if your DSRP refuses to cooperate, shows a lack of regard for research-based best practices, and/or threatens to charge you for content changes. The "Work With Your DSRP" chapter will also cover reasons why you might nonetheless need a workaround in the meantime. Thus, if you are

Tools

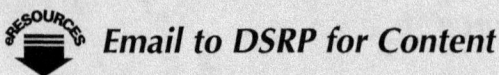 *Email to DSRP for Content*

Dear Data System/Report Provider,

I noticed our district's data system and reports do not adhere to the Over-the-Counter Data *Content* Standards that stipulate research-based practices for including effective and timely content in education data reports. Adherence to these *Content* standards is necessary to best support educators' easy use and thorough understanding of reports' data. Consider:

- Students, parents, teachers, and administrators need data presented in a way that clearly answers questions being posed and points toward a specific action within the data consumer's means (U.S. Department of Education Office of Educational Technology, 2012).
- Education data reporting tools should provide the information users need, when they need it, and in the format they need; hundreds of reports is overwhelming, difficult to use, and does not meet specific user needs (SAS Institute, 2013).
- The timeliness of score reporting is critical to a data source's ability to impact instruction (Faxon-Mills, Hamilton, Rudnick, & Stecher, 2013).

Please attune our data system/reports to adhere to the research-based Over-the-Counter Data *Content* Standards. These resources can help you:

- Over-the-Counter Data Standards are available with other eResources (including details on the research behind each standard) at www.routledge.com/9781138956155 (the *Content* standards are on pages 11–12, followed by a paper with related research).

- Read the book *Designing Data Reports that Work: A Guide for Creating Data Systems in Schools and Districts*, by Dr. Jenny Grant Rankin. This guide explains how to implement each reporting standard within a data system/report (offering specific examples, illustrations, etc.).

Thank you very much for your time and assistance. Adhering to these standards will offer tremendous help to educators and students.

—Me

Faxon-Mills, S., Hamilton, L. S., Rudnick, M., & Stecher, B. M. (2013). *New assessments, better instruction? Designing assessment systems to promote instructional improvement.* Santa Monica, CA: The RAND Corporation. Retrieved from www.rand.org/pubs/research_reports/RR354.html

SAS Institute. (2013). *Best practices in information management, reporting and analytics for education.* Retrieved from https://fs24.formsite.com/edweek/form15/secure_index.html

U.S. Department of Education Office of Educational Technology. (2012). *Enhancing teaching and learning through educational data mining and learning analytics: An issue brief.* Washington, DC: Author.

sure "the best approach" shared earlier has not worked for you and you are up for this more tedious (and thus less desirable) approach, here are some tips to help you compensate for common content problems:

- **If your DSRP is cooperative but content still falls short** (meaning your DSRP is aware of the OTCD Standards and is making changes to its report content, but the changes are not resulting in a comprehensive *and* streamlined suite of reports), your DSRP likely needs help understanding your needs. For example, a common problem is the DSRP tries to accommodate content needs by simply adding more and more data reports rather than reworking the suite as a whole so reports are consolidated where appropriate and kept to a manageable number.

Tools

> ### *Time-Saving Resource*
>
> The sample needs matrix (shown earlier in this chapter) can be downloaded and modified to suit your district's needs.

In this case, you can inquire as to whether or not your DSRP is working with a needs matrix and ask for a copy. Your next step can be to use the DSRP's needs matrix as a starting point (if one is available), or use the sample needs matrix provided earlier in this chapter as a starting point, in order to craft your own needs matrix. You can download this book's sample needs matrix and modify it to suit your school district's needs.

Be sure to involve key school district stakeholders in this process. Reference bullets 1–4 in the next section ("If You Provide Your Own Data System/Reports") offer guidance.

When the matrix is complete, share it with your DSRP and highlight any discrepancies between your needs and the data system's report offerings. This should help your DSRP better understand how its report suite can be improved. Even if your DSRP does not use your needs matrix, however, the matrix can serve as an important tool for:

- helping your district leaders understand the degree to which your data system reports do (and/or do not) align with your district's needs. If major deficiencies in the report offering persist, this can inform a decision to look for a new DSRP.

- helping your district leaders understand which reports are needed but missing so that supplemental reports can be created. The next bullet can help in this regard.

- **If there is a small amount of report content missing** (meaning some specific data should be added to reports that are otherwise effective, or a few key reports are missing from the suite of reports the data system offers), try persuading your DSRP again. However, while using a similar approach to that covered in the previous "The Best Approach" section, consider trying just one request at a time so the task does not seem overwhelming to your DSRP. Prioritize the changes you want (placing those most needed and/or easiest to implement at the top of your list), submit your top request, and then submit the next request after the previous one is granted.

If your DSRP still will not make the changes, many data systems still offer you the option of building your own custom reports. This option might involve using the product's business intelligence (BI) tool or custom report builder. If the data system will only allow you to select data for a simple tabular display, you can export the data you need into Microsoft® Excel and then use Excel's "Charts" feature and other tools to create more user-friendly reports. You can even use the same chart/file to copy/paste different datasets (i.e., from reports generated in different ways, such as for different teachers or students), and the charts will automatically update without your having to rebuild them. More help with Excel chart building can be found at office.microsoft.com/en-us/excel-help.

If You Provide Your Own Data System/Reports

If you provide your own data system/and or reports, you are in luck. You have direct control over the content in your staff's reporting environment. This section can also help if you provide just some of your own reports, such as building custom reports to supplement those that your data system offers prebuilt.

The following steps and tools will help you ensure your data reports, as well as the report suite as a whole, contain effective content:

1. Work with key stakeholders at your district to create a needs matrix that best reflects your district's data reporting needs. This team should involve varied roles (e.g., teacher leaders, assistant principals, data coaches, district admins) to be sure all roles' needs are reflected in the matrix. You can use the sample needs matrix as a starting point.

Tools

> ### *Plenty of Help*
>
> Your DSRP (or anyone else creating content for data reports) can use:
>
> - "Content" chapter in *Designing Data Reports that Work: A Guide for Creating Data Systems in Schools and Districts* (containing a lesson for implementing each OTCD Content standard).
> - The sample needs matrix (shown earlier in this chapter) can be downloaded and modified.

2. Working with the same team, identify ways in which your current report offering differs from the matrix:

Table 7.2

Shortcoming	Possible Fix
Needed reports are missing	Consider adding these reports and/or modifying existing reports
Content is missing from existing reports	Consider adding this content to existing reports
Reports that are not needed are present in report suite	Consider consolidating and/or removing reports
Content that is not needed is present in existing reports	Consider removing this content

3. Reference the "Content" chapter in *Designing Data Reports that Work: A Guide for Creating Data Systems in Schools and Districts*. The lessons in this chapter explain how to best implement each *Content* standard (offering specific examples, before and after illustrations, etc.). If you want a summary of research behind each *Content* standard, read the research information available.

4. Using the above resources, implement data report content that conforms to specific OTCD Standards.

References

Davis, M. R. (2013, October 1). Managing the digital district: Intelligent data analysis helps predict needs. *Education Week, 33*(6), 20–21. Bethesda, MD: Editorial Projects in Education.

Faxon-Mills, S., Hamilton, L. S., Rudnick, M., & Stecher, B. M. (2013). *New assessments, better instruction? Designing assessment systems to promote instructional improvement.* Santa Monica, CA: The RAND Corporation. Retrieved from www.rand.org/pubs/research_reports/RR354.html

SAS Institute. (2013). *Best practices in information management, reporting and analytics for education.* Retrieved from www.fs24.formsite.com/edweek/form15/secure_index.html

Tally, S. (2013, September 25). Purdue software boosts graduation rate 21 percent. *Purdue News.* West Lafayette, IN: Purdue University.

U.S. Department of Education Office of Educational Technology. (2012). *Enhancing teaching and learning through educational data mining and learning analytics: An issue brief.* Washington, DC: Author.

Work With Your DSRP

DSRPs Care about Students and Educators

Many educators have a distrust of edtech vendors such as data system/report providers (DSRPs), sometimes assuming these companies care more about profit than students or educators. While I have known some DSRPs to prioritize profit, the vast majority of DSRPs with which I'm familiar care more about students and educators than anyone or anything else. I have worked for a data system company staffed with great minds who work tirelessly for the users and students they serve. I have consulted data system companies who are passionate about applying research so their products can best help stakeholders.

Your DSRP *wants* to do a good job. Your DSRP *wants* to help you, your staff, and your students. You are on the same side, and if friction develops between you and your DSRP it can likely be remedied. This chapter will support you in maintaining a successful relationship with your DSRP team.

Recognize Your Power Over Change

Most educator leaders are using a data system that is provided by a third party (such as a vendor or, in rarer cases, a department within the district where the data system was custom built particularly for that district). Even if you are not employed within this company or department, there are still many occasions in which an educator leader such as yourself has the power to influence your data system. The "School District's Opportunities to Influence DSRP" diagram illustrates key opportunities when your DSRP is dependent on meeting your expressed needs:

- **District Issues RFP**—When your district is looking to purchase a new data system, the RFP likely released by your district will outline your district's specific data system requirements (e.g., product must allow users to create custom reports). Learning what product elements are vital to its purchase, the DSRP can be motivated to enhance its product to meet specifications.

> A **Request for Proposals (RFP)** is a solicitation an institution releases when the institution is seeking to purchase or employ a product or service, such as a new data system. Companies, organizations, or individuals seeking to be selected as the provider of this product or service each apply by submitting a proposal that meets the RFP's submission criteria. Learn more about RFPs in this book's glossary (available at wwww.routledge.com/9781138956155).

- **District Reviews Products**—There are often phases to the data system selection progress, where vendors do (or do not) advance to further stages. Whenever a DSRP is eliminated or advances to a new review phase, the district can share why this choice was made. This can enhance the DSRP community's understanding of product needs.
- **District Chooses Product**—When a data system wins a bid, DSRPs can learn which factors tipped the scales. Selection can also hinge on specific product enhancements. The district has the power to stand firm on elements crucial to making data work for staff.
- **District Uses Product**—As a district uses its data system, educator leaders should encourage users to share needs, concerns, and requests with them. Educator leaders should summarize these needs for other educator leaders within the district and with the DSRP's account managers and leaders to advocate for change. A good DSRP will try its best to evaluate and accommodate favorable enhancements.
- **District Replaces Product**—If a DSRP fails to meet a district's needs and is replaced, the DSRP can learn the importance of district needs that were not met.

Maintain a Successful Relationship with Your DSRP

DSRPs typically plan enhancements to their products based on what educators—being the clients and users—request. There is often an assumption by DSRPs that most of clients' needs are contained within clients' requests. Thus many DSRPs do not follow the latest over-the-counter data (OTCD) research. They often follow design literature, such as that involved in OTCD *Package/Display* standards, but that addresses only one-fifth of OTCD components necessary to make data fully work. Even then, educators represent specific users that sometimes deviate from the user that most design literature is written to support.

> ## Working With DSRP
>
> - Know who/how to contact
> - Prioritize requests
> - Give specifics
> - Respect your DSRP's expertise
> - Nurture the relationship
> - Follow up as necessary.

Of course, most educators are too busy to read the latest research on the best ways to report data. Thus requests that adhere to research on making data work are typically missing from the requests educators make of their DSRPs. You have this book to change that dynamic.

Many of this book's chapters culminate with emails you can send to your DSRP to spark changes that will make your data easy for staff to understand and use. The following guidelines for working with your DSRP can increase this contact's success.

Know Who/How to Contact

Determine the best way to communicate with your DSRP. Some districts or DSRPs require modification requests to go through a particular district administrator, and you will want to adhere to established protocol. In most cases it is appropriate for you to communicate with your DSRP directly, but even then you will want to understand who at the DSRP is the best contact. This person could be the Customer Service Department, but there is likely an implementation manager or other team member through whom you will find faster results. The stronger a relationship you establish with your contact, the better.

Sometimes it is an advantage if district administrators also contact the DSRP advocating for the same change(s). Sometimes the more colleagues you can get to request the same enhancements, the better, as this can help raise the DSRP's awareness of research-based best practices while also encouraging the DSRP to make your request a priority. Talk with the district leader who oversees the data system at your district in order to follow the most effective communication protocol. Also speak with educator leaders at other districts who use the same product. They could be in a position to advocate for change, as well.

Prioritize Requests

The main reason it is recommended you read this book in its entirety before contacting your DSRP is the need to prioritize requests. There is a chance your data system is deficient in multiple OTCD areas. For example, you might find that effective labels, supplemental documentation, and a help system are all missing from your data system.

If you bombard your DSRP with multiple emails featuring different requests, it will be hard for your DSRP to target your needs in the best order possible. Instead, identify areas in which your data system needs to improve and consult with key stakeholders at your district concerning how these changes should be prioritized. For example, your district's grade/department chairs and administrators might concur the data reports' display is confusing teachers, and this is the biggest problem, though improved labeling and supplemental documentation could also help. The "Evaluate Your Data Tool" section earlier in this book can help.

Tools

> ### *Time-Saving Resource*
>
> Copy/paste text from the email below into your own email. You might also use the Educational Leader's Evaluation of Data System/Report Tool (explained in the "Tool Evaluation" section).

Rather than sending your DSRP a string of emails, consolidate your needs into a single email to initiate changes to your data system/reports. This book makes it easy for you to request multiple OTCD Standards by providing an already-written email (shown below) you can send to your data system/report provider (DSRP). The email is even provided for you at *overthecounterdata.com/edsall*, so you can simply copy/paste the text into an email and modify/personalize your message as needed.

You will want to add specifics to this email, as covered in the next section. For example, it could help to highlight a single request you would like your DSRP to begin with. Prioritize the changes you want (placing those most needed and/or easiest to implement at the top of your list), submit your top request, and then submit the next request once the previous one is granted.

Email to DSRP for All Standards

Dear Data System/Report Provider,

I noticed our district's data reports do not adhere to the Over-the-Counter Data Standards that stipulate research-based ways to report data to educators. Adherence to these standards is necessary to best support educators' easy use and thorough understanding of reports' data. Consider:

- Only 48% of teachers' inferences based on given data are accurate at districts with strong data cultures (U.S. Department of Education

Office of Planning, Evaluation and Policy Development, 2009), with other educators' analyses being less accurate.

- Adhering to some Over-the-Counter Data Standards can *triple* or even *quadruple* educators' data analysis accuracy (Rankin, 2013).

Please attune our data system/reports to adhere to the research-based Over-the-Counter Data Standards. These resources can help you:

- Over-the-Counter Data Standards (and a paper on the research behind them) are available with other eResources at www.routledge.com/9781138956155.
- Read the book *Designing Data Reports that Work: A Guide for Creating Data Systems in Schools and Districts*, by Dr. Jenny Grant Rankin. This guide explains how to implement each reporting standard within a data system/reports (offering specific examples, before and after illustrations, etc.).
- Free templates and examples (for reference sheets and reference guides) that are aligned to Over-the-Counter Data Standards and the supplemental documentation shown to be effective in the Rankin study are also available with other eResources at www.routledge.com/9781138956155.

Thank you very much for your time and assistance. Adhering to these standards will offer tremendous help to educators and students.

—Me

Rankin, J. G. (2013). *Over-the-counter data's impact on educators' data analysis accuracy.* ProQuest Dissertations and Theses, 3575082. Retrieved from http://pqdtopen.proquest.com/doc/1459258514.html?FMT=ABS

U.S. Department of Education Office of Planning, Evaluation and Policy Development. (2009). *Implementing data-informed decision making in schools: Teacher access, supports and use.* United States Department of Education (ERIC Document Reproduction Service No. ED504191).

Tools

Give Specifics

The pre-written emails provided in this book and at overthecounterdata.com/makedatawork can alert your DSRP to widespread problems and instigate the data system's adherence to OTCD Standards. However, providing your DSRP with specific examples of what you see (versus what you *need* to see) in the data system can help in two scenarios:

- **The Data System Mostly Makes Data Work**—There might be only a few instances in which your data system is not adhering to OTCD Standards. For example, most of the data reports might employ effective package/display except for two or three reports.

  In these cases, let your DSRP know that only a few instances need remedying. Use the provided email so your DSRP understands your request's importance, but modify the email to:

  - Make it clear your DSRP is doing a great job and only a few instances need to be fixed. This will increase your DSRP's likelihood of viewing your request as a manageable task to complete.
  - Provide specifics on the changes that need to be made.

- **The Data System Mostly Does Not Make Data Work**—When your data system is generally *not* adhering to OTCD Standards, it is especially important for you to use the provided email. This will alert your DSRP to the problem and its impact, as well as resources that can help fix it. To make the email more effective, you can accompany it with specific examples.

  Note this email will work best if you include a request to discuss any major problems in person with key DSRP representatives who can improve the situation. At the very least, talk with your DSRP contact over the phone to get the ball rolling. The stronger your relationship with your DSRP, the greater your chances of provoking change, and non-written communication can assist this relationship.

In either of the above cases, the following tips can help you include a specific example in your email to your DSRP:

- Provide a screenshot of the area in the data system where the problem appears. The table below will help you take a screenshot, which involves saving a picture of what your screen looks like so you can send that picture file to your DSRP.
- Describe where the problem occurs in the data system (it sometimes helps to provide the URL that appears when you are on a specific screen).
- Explain what you see in the data system versus what you need to see and why (e.g., what you are trying to achieve, or how the current function impacts data use).
- If the problem involves an action, describe the current process (e.g., what you are clicking, step by step).

Table 8.1

Computer	How to Take a Screenshot
Mac	On your keyboard, simultaneously press *Command* (⌘), *Shift*, and *3*. This will save (to your desktop) a screenshot of everything you see on your computer screen. To save an image of just a portion of your screen, simultaneously press *Command* (⌘), *Shift*, and *4*, then select a screen area using your mouse.
Windows	On your keyboard, simultaneously press *Ctrl*, *Alt*, and *Print Screen* (sometimes abbreviated as *Prtsc*). This will save a screenshot to your clipboard, which you can then paste in a program like Microsoft Word by simultaneously pressing *Ctrl* and *V* on your keyboard. Save that file by simultaneously pressing *Ctrl* and *S* on your keyboard.
Windows (newer editions, such as Windows 7 and later)	On your screen, click *Start* and then type snipping in the search field. All Programs. Click *Snipping Tool* when you see it appear at the top of the window. Click (and hold down your click) to select the part of the screen you want to save. When you let go, you can click *File* and then *Save As* within the Snipping Tool window to save your screenshot.

Provide any examples or details to help the DSRP spot the problem (e.g., "If you generate the 2015 *Class Roster* report for teacher *Kurt Lecture* at *Earl. E. Learner Elementary*, notice how student *Val A. Dictorian* shows 105 percent for attendance when such a record is not possible").

Respect Your DSRP's Expertise

Just as you want your DSRP to respect your expertise as an educator, you should respect your DSRP's expertise in technology and data, as well as your DSRP's expertise in working with a large number of school districts. Some OTCD Standards may be harder to implement within some data systems than others, due to the data system's unique technological makeup and the DSRP's unique staff, business structure, and commitments.

On the one hand, you should not let yourself be strong-armed by a DSRP who trivializes your requests or does not want to invest the effort in adhering to research-based standards. However, you also want to listen to any DSRP concerns, such as limitations in its system due to technology already laid as its foundation. When both sides work together to pursue what is best for the system, you will all have the advantage of both sides' expertise.

Nurture the Relationship

Think of the people you work best with at your school or school district. Reflect on how that relationship works. You likely respect one another's views and feelings, are sensitive to one another's time and time restraints, and enjoy a healthy give-and-take that allows you to accomplish more together than either of you could on your own.

The same dynamic is true of healthy relations between DSRPs and educators. View the DSRP as an extension of your district: like a department that operates by separate rules but still plays an important role in getting things done for the good of students. Do what you can to forge and maintain a strong relationship with each DSRP representative you interact with, and you will likely see an impact on how well your DSRP responds to your needs.

Experience from the Field

"Why bother with building a relationship with your data system/report provider (DSRP)? After selecting our K-12 school district's DSRP, we began to build a relationship that quickly evolved into a true collaborative partnership. While it was in the DSRP's best interests to become familiar with our school district's data and reporting needs, it was also important for our school district to recognize the needs and goals of the DSRP. For example, at the beginning of our relationship with the DSRP, we identified the types of pre-built reports currently available within the data and reporting system and suggested the development of additional reports needed for instructional planning and program evaluation. Responding to our requests for customized reports and new features strengthened the DSRP's product, which helped them attract new clients, and which in turn generated even more new ideas for product development and system enhancements.

One simple step can strengthen the relationship with your DSRP and provide school district staff with a deeper understanding of the data and reporting system's features. Our DSRP held quarterly user meetings and annual conferences during which many school districts using the same product could collaborate, learn from each other, and offer suggestions for system improvements. You can support your DSRP and grow professionally by participating in or presenting at user meetings and conferences. Sharing your experiences and knowledge will help other professionals in your position, and your participation will help the DSRP improve its product and services."

—Sharon Cordes, Ed.D., Director, Assessment and Evaluation, Tustin Unified School District

Follow up as Necessary

The pre-written emails provided in this book can ignite dialogue and initiate important first steps to improving the data reporting environment you and your staff use. However, face-to-face conversations and follow-ups can be immensely effective in maintaining the momentum of change.

Follow up with your DSRP as time allows and encourage your colleagues to add their voices to the movement as needed. The goal should never be to *hound* your DSRP, as positive relations with your DSRP are paramount and you do not want to waste your DSRP's time with unnecessary dialogue. However, your colleagues' added voices can be an important tool to employ if you sense your needs are being overlooked or trivialized. Checking in with your DSRP's progress on specific changes also provides you with an opportunity to offer your help (e.g., clarification regarding your needs, resources you have found to be helpful, etc.), thus speeding your data system's improvement.

When your report environment is improved, thank those involved for making a big difference for users and students. Even if your data system is not perfect (as none are), as long as those who use it and those who offer it are working together in earnest to improve data reporting, and value one another's roles in this endeavor, you are well on your way to reaping the benefits of making data truly work for educators.

If You Hit a Wall

As wonderful as most DSRP team members are, no field is without exceptions. Refusal to cooperate, showing a lack of regard for research-based best practices, and/or threatening to charge you for necessary changes to the reporting environment would all be reasons to consider adopting a different data system when your contract with the DSRP comes up for renewal. It is better to acquire a DSRP who will adhere to the research-based OTCD Standards rather than trying to "work around" this obstacle.

Selecting a New Data System

If your district decides to replace your data system, key staff will want to evaluate potential data systems in order to select one that communicates most effectively (i.e., best assists data analysis ease and accuracy).

- Write an OTCD Standards segment into your Request for Proposals (RFP).
- Use this book while evaluating potential data systems' adherence to OTCD Standards.
- RFP Committee members with a good understanding of OTCD (e.g., who have read this book) can share and discuss OTCD RFP segment findings with the rest of the RFP Committee.
- Commentary related to the above should be added to any records communicating how the data system selection process transpired.

Of course, we educators are masters of making something undesirable work for us if need be. Sometimes you are stuck with a data system due to district politics, or sometimes you have the right data system but have to wait an extended period for improvements. "The Less Desirable Approach" section recommendations throughout this book are appropriate for such occasions and put the power of making data work in your own, capable educator hands.

Even when you have a great DSRP who values your feedback for product improvement, you might still run into obstacles. If left unchecked, poor or unproductive educator/DSRP relations can undermine your attempts to acquire data that works for you and your staff. The following table offers guidelines for navigating common dilemmas if they arise.

Table 8.2

Dilemma	Proactive Response
You run into a standard your DSRP does not think it can implement.	Even if your DSRP cannot implement some OTCD Standards due to the technology your data system uses or other reason(s), you can still **benefit from other standards**. Ask, "What *can* my DSRP implement?" and encourage your DSRP to work on that. Your system will not have all of the standards' benefits if it does not follow all standards, but it's better for educators and students if it has as many as possible. Hopefully, you can rectify remaining standards in the future.
There is friction between the two camps: educators and DSRPs.	Be sure everyone involved shares a **common understanding** of: • how widespread data analysis errors are; • the evidence this book's standards improve education data reporting to help eliminate widespread data analysis errors; • the impact various system design decisions have on educators' data analyses and thus students. Any resistant educator leaders should read this book or at least its introduction to gain the above understanding. Any resistant DSRPs should read *Designing Data Reports that Work: A Guide for Creating Data Systems in Schools and Districts*, by Dr. Jenny Grant Rankin to gain the above understanding. Remind those involved of your **shared goal** to help students. Reiterate you are on the same team. If necessary, collaborate on positive communication guidelines. Be sure each camp is thoroughly listening to **the other camp's concerns**.
You suspect the aforementioned friction is related to gender issues.	Given the significant gender differences prevalent between data system users/educators (disproportionately female) and data system DSRPs (disproportionately male), gender issues are especially relevant to OTCD implementation:

Table 8.2 Continued

Dilemma	Proactive Response
... Continued	- **Educators**—Data systems' leading consumers are female; the U.S. Dept. of Education's National Center for Education Statistics reports 75% of all teachers are women (Papay, Harvard Graduate School of Education, 2007). - **DSRPs**—Only 22% of computer programmers and 21% of computer software engineers (i.e., the roles commonly involved in building reports in education data systems) are female (U.S. Department of Labor, U.S. Bureau of Labor Statistics, 2011). If gender issues arise, all parties intimately involved with the report suite can read Sheryl Sandberg's *Lean In* (at least chapters 1–3 and 10) to expand understanding of current gender issues impacting communication. Discussion should ensue, as should deliberate and active steps to best ensure the gender differences common in DSRP–educator correspondence do not undermine the data system's reflection of educator and researcher input. Both genders contribute to gender issues, and those who feel they demonstrate no gender bias can actually be more likely to demonstrate gender bias due to what's known as a "bias blind spot" (Sandberg, 2013). Many development and reporting debacles occur with data systems because of miscommunication between educators and DSRPs: some because a voice was misunderstood, and some because a voice was never fully heard in the first place. Both genders can take steps to improve communication between educators and edtech, regardless of the side on which they work, as well as within their own workplaces.

Conclusion

In an issue brief on using educational data mining and analytics to improve teaching and learning, the U.S. Department of Education Office of Educational Technology (2012):

- called for better collaboration between the research, commercial, and educational communities in order to co-design the best educational technology tools;
- called on educators to ask critical questions about commercial offerings and purchase intelligently in order to create demand for the most useful educational technology features and uses;
- called on researchers and technology developers to conduct research concerning the effectiveness and usability of data displays.

None of this can be achieved—nor can its benefits—without all stakeholders working together for the common good. We are all in this together, and input from all stakeholders is needed to refine tools that can best help students.

References

Papay, J., Harvard Graduate School of Education. (2007). *Aspen Institute datasheet: The teaching workforce.* Washington, DC: The Aspen Institute.

Rankin, J. G. (2013). *Over-the-counter data's impact on educators' data analysis accuracy.* ProQuest Dissertations and Theses, 3575082. Retrieved from pqdtopen.proquest.com/doc/1459258514.html?FMT=ABS

Sandberg, S. (2013). *Lean in: Women, work, and the will to lead.* New York, NY: Alfred A. Knopf.

U.S. Department of Education Office of Educational Technology. (2012). *Enhancing teaching and learning through educational data mining and learning analytics: An issue brief.* Washington, DC: Author.

U.S. Department of Education Office of Planning, Evaluation and Policy Development. (2009). *Implementing data-informed decision making in schools: Teacher access, supports and use.* United States Department of Education (ERIC Document Reproduction Service No. ED504191).

U.S. Department of Labor, U.S. Bureau of Labor Statistics. (2011, July). *Highlights of women's earnings in 2010: Report 1031.* Retrieved from www.bls.gov/cps/cpswom2009.pdf

PART III

Climate

> When we try to pick out anything by itself, we find it hitched to everything else in the Universe.
>
> —John Muir

Other Pieces to Make Data Work

The National Center for Education Statistics estimates less than 2 percent of school districts in the USA, which total over 13,000, are able to turn the data languishing in data warehouses into information that educators can use (Sparks, 2014). Yikes! Most educator leaders ignore the value of shaping the data itself into a format that is easy to understand and use. You can be the exception if you advocate for improved data tools and data (covered in the previous "Tools" section).

As covered in the second chapter, most school districts rely exclusively on professional development (PD) and staff supports (strong leadership, data coaches, PLCs, collaboration, etc.) to improve staff's data use. Exclusively relying on only one means for improving data use ignores vital components to making data work and fails to prevent staff from struggling. For example, in a study where teachers received PD in educational measurement/ assessment, all teachers struggled afterwards with statistical terms and measurement concepts (Zapata-Rivera & VanWinkle, 2010).

Does this mean PD and improved climate are bad? No way. Many research findings indicate these factors are vital to successful data use. So . . .

Now that you have used the "Tools" section of this book to improve your data reporting environment, your other efforts to improve your staff's data use can flourish. However, seeing to your staff's needs is a tricky business. The next two chapters will offer you support by summarizing the large body of literature on maximizing the remaining elements involved in making data work for staff: data use climate and data users.

My outlook tends to be more Pollyannaish than Machiavellian. However, the following excerpt from *The Prince* by Niccolò Machiavelli sure does capture the potential hazards of advocating for significant change within a school or school district:

> There is nothing more difficult to take in hand, more perilous to conduct, or more uncertain in its success, than to take the lead in the introduction of a new order of things. Because the innovator has for enemies all those who have done well under the old conditions, and lukewarm defenders in those who may do well under the new.

Following guidelines shown to be successful thus becomes vital when championing changes within a data climate or data users. The next chapter will help you maximize staff's data use climate, whereas the next section ("Data Users") will help you best train and support your data-using staff.

What Is Climate?

Climate refers to the conditions under which staff works, and this climate is influenced by school and district data cultures and mandates. In Wayman's (2005) review of data use research, educator leaders' provision of a supportive data use climate, which involves opportunities for collaboration, ties with professional development as the top support that teachers require when using data systems. Apply this and the next chapter's tips to your own efforts in establishing a productive climate for data use.

Evaluate Your Data Use Climate

Evaluating your district's, site's, or group's data use climate can help you plan appropriate steps to facilitate any necessary improvements. Online resources can assist your evaluation, and you can choose the format(s) you prefer:

> ### Time-Saving Resource
>
> Use the evaluations described here in whichever format you prefer (online survey vs. Word document):
>
> - Educational Leader's Evaluation of Site's Data Use Climate
> - Staff's Evaluation of Site's Data Use Climate

- **Online climate evaluation (in survey format) you can complete** to receive results (and an evaluation score) automatically emailed to you;
- **Online climate evaluation (in survey format) staff can complete** to enhance your understanding of staff perception; when staff completes this evaluation using your email address, results (and an evaluation score) will be automatically emailed to you every time another staff member completes the form; a better option is to copy/paste these evaluation questions into a new, single survey form you manage (using a tool like Google Doc Forms or SurveyMonkey) so all staff members' responses can be easily aggregated.
- **Word file of climate evaluation (which you can edit as necessary to suit your site) you can complete** on your computer or in printed form to evaluate your site's climate while also adding notes concerning steps you plan to take to improve areas (which the next chapter will help you determine).

- **Word file of climate evaluation (which you can edit as necessary to suit your site) staff can complete** to enhance your understanding of staff perception; staff can complete this in hard copy format, or you can copy/paste these evaluation questions into a new, single survey form you manage so all staff members' responses can be easily aggregated.

While completing one of the above evaluations, refer to this book as necessary (particularly the next chapter) to better understand any of the evaluation's questions.

Use the evaluation in whatever way is most helpful for you. For example, you and your colleagues might discuss and complete the evaluation as a district department, or you might reflect on all of the evaluation's questions by yourself and write notes beside each question.

Determining what constitutes a "yes" versus a "no" on the evaluation should be based on what you (or the group with which you are working) deem to be desirable yet reasonable for your site's current stage of data use. Determine what level of adherence constitutes a "Yes" answer versus a "No" answer before beginning the evaluation. For example:

- At an early stage of site-wide data use you might answer "yes" to a question of whether or not staff feels a particular way based on at least 65 percent of your staff sharing that feeling. However, a site at an advanced stage of data use might warrant at least 90 percent before answering "yes" to that same question.

You can return to this survey as often as you like to re-evaluate your climate over time.

References

Sparks, S. D. (2014, July 25). Can states make student data useful for schools? *Education Week*. Retrieved from blogs.edweek.org/edweek/inside-school-research/2014/07/can_states_turn_slag_data_into.html

Wayman, J. C. (2005). Involving teachers in data-driven decision making: Using computer data systems to support teacher inquiry and reflection. *Journal of Education for Students Placed At Risk, 10*(3), 295–308.

Zapata-Rivera, D., & VanWinkle, W. (2010). A research-based approach to designing and evaluating score reports for teachers. *ETS Research Memorandum. RM-10–01*. Princeton, NJ: ETS.

Climate Maximization

How to Maximize Climate

Improving the conditions under which staff uses data is an ongoing, multifaceted process. This chapter contains strategies most important to that process, as well as strategies most frequently neglected by educator leaders. By employing each of these strategies (and/or advocating for leaders above you to apply them), you can maximize your climate's chances of helping data work for staff.

Start an Urgency Fire, but Make It a Controlled Burn

"By far the biggest mistake people make when trying to change organizations is to plunge ahead without establishing a high enough sense of urgency in fellow managers and employees" (Kotter, 1996, p. 4). You need to help staff realize the importance of using data to help each student succeed. Data can be a powerful tool in illustrating this urgency. For example, share straightforward data with staff indicating the school's EL students' language and math skills are regressing, or share student survey data indicating students do not feel engaged in their classes.

The goal is to get staff fired up enough to advance their data use and push through the growing pains of change. However, the fire you start should be a controlled burn. You do not want to discourage staff or throw staff into a panic, which can be easy when staff is already overwhelmed with the mountain of demands educators juggle. The remaining tips in this section will help.

Use Data Responsibly

Some educator leaders have used value-added models (VAMs) to rate teachers based on how their students scored on standardized tests (in relation to how the VAM formula projects each student should have scored based on prior assessments). These VAM ratings are used to measure each teacher's effectiveness in rendering student achievement. Some school districts have even publicly released individual teachers' VAM ratings (see Song & Felch, 2011). This famously resulted in widespread humiliation, outrage, and even one teacher's suicide.

As convenient as it could be to have a single score capturing a teacher's effectiveness, VAM is not this powerful. There are simply too many variables at play to conclude a VAM score directly reflects how good a teacher was at doing his or her job. The American Statistical Association (ASA) (2014, p. 2) said it best when they released the *ASA Statement on Using Value-Added Models for Educational Assessment* and listed these limitations:

- VAMs are generally based on standardized test scores, and do not directly measure potential teacher contributions toward other student outcomes.
- VAMs typically measure correlation, not causation: Effects—positive or negative—attributed to a teacher may actually be caused by other factors that are not captured in the model.
- Under some conditions, VAM scores and rankings can change substantially when a different model or test is used, and a thorough analysis should be undertaken to evaluate the sensitivity of estimates to different models.

Does this mean you cannot use data to better understand teacher effectiveness? *It does not.* Data can be a powerful tool in identifying areas in which teachers might need to improve. However, "teacher performance" data is not foolproof (and thus should never be treated as such), and it should be just one indicator of many used, with a thorough understanding of other variables that might have impacted the data. For example:

- The teacher who is a superstar with English Learners and thus welcomes many into her classroom mid-year can look like her class's scores dropped.
- At lower grade levels, the teacher who has mastered "drill and kill" instruction can look great on paper but sends his kids off to the next grade unable to tackle abstract thinking and open-ended problem solving.
- In honors classes, students entering at the advanced level cannot show improvement and contribute to an impression that performance has dropped in those classes as there are no score improvements to counterbalance scores that drop.

Data should be treated as a tool to support teachers and their students—not to rob teachers of professional dignity. Likewise, it is counterproductive to force the transparency of scores before each group of teachers is ready for it. The more you treat data as something positive, which you and your staff can use to get even better while also celebrating strengths, the more your staff will embrace data and benefit from its use. See "Sample Data Types to Support Data Analyses" and "Sample Questions Data Can Help Answer" to guide discussions concerning positive uses of data.

Involve Staff in Planning Processes

In the National Longitudinal Evaluation of Comprehensive School Reform, it was found when staff members are involved at the onset of an adoption of a comprehensive school reform, their involvement is likely to foster a climate in which teachers are united behind a common goal (Aladjem et al., 2006). United efforts also make it easier to promote use of a common language surrounding data use, which is essential to promoting an effective data culture (Wohlstetter, Datnow, & Park, 2008).

Use systems for regularly capturing staff feedback, and apply this feedback to your decision-making. For example:

- If you are a district administrator, survey staff two to four times per year to assess needs, concerns, and successes involving data use. Use this

Checklist for Improving Data Use Climate

- Start an urgency fire, but make it a controlled burn
- Use data responsibly
- Involve staff in planning processes
- Have a plan to replicate what is working
- Do not bury staff in data busywork
- Data use is integrated—not "one more thing"
- Give the gift of time
- Be a strong data leader
- Test conservatively.

Free and Easy Ways to Survey Your Staff

- Google Docs (using the Forms feature) www.google.com/forms/about
- SurveyMonkey www.surveymonkey.com
- Your data system might include a feature that can be used to survey staff (such as its assessment tool).

feedback and conversations with school administrators to inform individualized professional development, next steps in your data plans, visitations between different schools' staff to learn from one another, and more.

- If you are a school administrator, hold weekly meetings with all your grade/department chairs or other leadership team and involve them in your school-wide plans for data.
- If you are a data coach or department chair, have one-on-one conversations with your colleagues where you ask for candid feedback

on how they view the school's or department's data use and what needs or concerns they might have. Work together on any needed solutions and involve other staff (e.g., a school's principal) as needed to ensure staff is supported.

Have a Plan to Replicate What Is Working

As staff uses multiple measures of data, successes will be spotted. For example, perhaps there are multiple indicators that English Learners in math teacher Hugh G. Cuajión's class are performing as well with word problems as their native English-speaking peers. Rather than just pat Hugh G. Cuajión on the back, you should have a clear system in place to help Hugh's colleagues apply whatever Hugh has likely found to be successful in helping English Learners master word problems.

> ### Too Much Caution
>
> In education, it is extremely difficult to prove causation (A caused B) over correlation (A and B both occurred, but A did not necessarily cause B). There are simply too many variables within classrooms and schools. Thus there will always be some degree of risk or flaw in educators' conclusions concerning what (e.g., a new lesson plan, an instructional strategy, etc.) caused an outcome (e.g., improved performance). The alternative to this risk is to never use data, or to never draw educated conclusions that have great potential to further best practices and end poor practices. Better your staff uses common sense and their professional judgment to learn likely scenarios from data and share this knowledge with their colleagues.

Make "share what is working" part of your school's or district's established approach for data use. When data indicates an educator or educator team is having success in a particular area, they should be expected to identify the likely cause (if possible), share this identification with their colleagues, and share any related resources (e.g., lesson plans, articles on a strategy, project assignments, etc.). This practice treats educators as the experts they are and also demonstrates confidence in their ability to identify the likely cause of an effect in the classroom.

In addition, this sharing practice should not be haphazard. There should be a single, established, web-based venue through which staff shares and accesses successful resources. For example, staff can add each successful resource to Activate Instruction (www.activateinstruction.org), a free tool where they can tag the resource by Common Core State Standards (CCSS), topic, critical thinking level, and more. This allows other educators, whether or not they are based at the same school site, to find the resource when they are searching for something of the same nature. Imagine the impact when educators across your district have fast and easy ways to apply the best lessons and strategies for any given topic.

Do Not Bury Staff in Data Busywork

Educators use the term *busywork* to refer to work given to students that is not as effective as it could be in rendering significant learning or advancement. Dry worksheets come to mind. "Busywork" likely bores students, might be given to them for work's sake, and often leaves students feeling like their time is wasted.

Busywork can also be given to *educators*, typically with the best intentions. Sadly, most busywork I have seen foisted upon educators relates to data use.

There are countless books on improving educators' data use. Most contain information of value to educator leaders, as reading such books will add to your arsenal of tools for supporting staff with ever-changing data needs. However, many of these books convey over-complicated approaches to data use. It's as if their authors think data use is the only topic in which educators must be experts, and/or the only professional endeavor to which educators must devote their time. Do not cause your staff to wonder if you have the same misunderstandings.

Educators should have more time to coordinate their data-informed actions than they spend dissecting the data that informs these actions. Otherwise, how is anyone supposed to benefit from the data? Knowing something but not having the time to do anything about it would be a tragedy.

Climate

Experience from the Field

"Building a true learning community within a school is never an easy task but is essential to the growth of each student. A culture where learning is the focus for every student as opposed to the *class average* can only be accomplished by creating a foundation based on KNOWING what students need. This knowing comes not from intuition but from data that objectively reports to teachers what students have actually learned, internalized.

How does one actually build that culture of learning for all? It begins with cultivating an understanding of data and (as critical) how to use that data to support student achievement. Not an easy task as many educators are fearful of data for many reasons. Often they lack an understanding, even a belief, in the assessment itself. This then negates the instructional value of the data. Thus it is essential that the school leader build a culture in which data is both understood and valued.

Creating a climate of "controlled urgency" is essential. A leader must teach and inspire staff to both understand and trust the data. Involving staff in the development and planning is fundamental to this process. If teachers understand and trust in the assessment tools then utilizing the data becomes a natural progression. This is a process which requires time, trust, open communication lines and an unfailing commitment by the school leader to continuously drive the process.

Celebrations of success must also become a part of this process. Creating opportunities for teachers to share what worked well is critical for providing on-site and – I might add – highly credible professional development as well as maximizing planning time for colleagues.

This chapter is a definite must read for any school leader looking to build a school-wide learning culture focused on growth for *every child (student) every day!*"

—Debra L. Diaz, Principal
Charles G. Emery Elementary School

Climate Maximization

Cut countless hours out of staff's data analysis time in these ways:

- **Give staff tools that make data work.** Staff should be able to easily find the data reports they need and easily understand the data's implications in these reports. This was covered in the "Tools" section of this book and cannot be over-emphasized.

- **Critically evaluate any data processes you ask of staff.** Consider tools like worksheets or graphic organizers you require staff to complete, procedural steps like questions PLCs are required to discuss, agendas like those required of department meetings, etc. Does the approach give staff enough bang (i.e., data-based understanding) for its buck (i.e., time and resources spent)? If it does not, find a way to make the process more efficient while maintaining the same benefit. Keep in mind that even if an extended process has theoretical benefit, that benefit cannot be reached when staff try to cut corners, tune out, and disengage in other ways because the process is overly taxing.

- **Keep data analyses focused.** When staff conducts a designated data analysis, it is overwhelming to try to tackle an unlimited number of questions. Have set goals for these analyses, such as understanding which standards are likely strengths and which are weaknesses for each teacher's students, a list of students in need of added intervention in a particular area, or how subgroups are progressing in relation to one another. Other topics can be tackled at other times, but educators have a better chance of reaching the prioritized analysis goal within the allotted time if they can focus on an established goal.

Data Use is Integrated—Not "One More Thing"

Many teachers report they do not have enough time for data analysis, and that completing data processes can come at the expense of delivering quality instruction due to the tradeoff of time (Ingram, Louis, & Schroeder, 2004). This problem is fueled by cases where data use is structured (and thus perceived) as yet "one more thing" educators have to "do" within their busy profession.

While many books (such as this one) are devoted primarily to the topic of data, there are surely many other topics being incorporated into your

Climate

Table 9.1

Endeavor	Point in Time	Infuse Data	"Aha!" for Staff
Response to Intervention (RTI)	Teachers discuss which students to "swap" for a reteach of a unit's concepts	Support teachers in using particular reports in the data system for this practice	"Using the data system instantly showed us likely ways to organize the reteach, and we even spotted cases where students needed to change RTI tiers! What a time-saver!"
Increasing student engagement and differentiating	Teachers are supposed to bring sample homework assignments to a PD session based on their likelihood of engaging students and accounting for different learning styles and preferences	Give teachers the five quick steps for running a report in which they can spot which homework assignment had the highest turn-in rate	"Using the data system I instantly saw which homework assignment was most popular with my students and considered why it was so appealing. It turned out to be my most engaging assignment and had options where students could choose the ways in which they completed the assignment. What a time-saver!"
Behavior Improvement Plans (BIPs)	A student's BIP will be discussed at an IEP.	Have the Special Education Department Chair help teachers generate behavior tracking reports for IEPs	"All stakeholders could easily see how the student was progressing with the behavior. I can't wait to also use the data system when performing a Functional Behavior Assessment, considering student data (behavioral, performance, health, etc.) when creating or modifying BIPs, etc. What a time-saver!"

staff's professional efforts. For example, maybe your site is implementing Response to Intervention (RTI), your teachers engage in PD for increasing student engagement and differentiating, staff is developing Behavior Improvement Plans (BIPs) for specific students, etc. In other words, you and your staff are inundated with topics on which you must be experts and to which you must devote your time. Data does not have to be one more obligation on an already towering stack.

Data should make all those other obligations easier. Infuse data use in other processes by building staff's capacity to use data for existing endeavors. See Table 9.1 for examples from the previous paragraph.

Note how data is infused into existing endeavors so that it saves educator time, and educators instantly benefit (not to mention their students benefit) from the data's use. This greatly increases the educator's chances of using the data again on his or her own, and the experience adds to the educator's positive perception of data and to related tools and processes.

Of course, data integration is not a magically positive experience. As an educator leader, you must take all steps necessary to ensure that it is a successful experience for educators. For example, if you ask that educators generate a particular data report for a task, pair your request with the five simple steps needed to generate the report (even if staff have been trained on how to do so), a link to the reference guide that explains how to read the report, and the name and contact information of the person teachers should talk to if they require any help with the task. Think of any confusion or need that might interfere with staff's incorporation of data and provide well-timed supports to overcome them.

Give the Gift of Time

A vital component to successful data use is time. Anderegg (2007); Bigger (2006); Datnow, Park, and Wohlstetter (2007); Wayman, Cho, and Johnston (2007); and Wayman and Stringfield (2006) all offer findings that staff needs designated, structured time to collaboratively work with student data and discuss the instructional changes this data informs. This time can sometimes be used for related professional development.

You might be wincing right now. Finding staff time for data use is one of the hardest tasks set before educator leaders. I will not pretend it is easy, but I will maintain that it is vital. Consider:

Climate

- Educators need time in order to know how to act on the data they view, and lack of such time is limiting the data's use at many sites, as few sites offer this critical component of data-informed decision-making (Marsh, Pane, & Hamilton, 2006).
- Teachers have very little time for data analysis, and this problem worsens as assessment frequency and complexity increases (Rennie Center for Education Research and Policy, 2006).
- Most teachers do not collaborate with others when using data, and many teachers do not have enough time to discuss data with others (Wayman, Cho, & Shaw, 2009).

The more you integrate data use with existing endeavors (see the previous section: Data Use is Integrated—Not "One More Thing") the easier this will be. The faster and simpler you make data use (see another previous section: Do Not Bury Staff in Data Busywork), such as by offering improved data tools, the easier this will be. However, there is no simple, single answer, as the best way to offer staff time for data differs by site.

See *Using Student Achievement Data to Support Instructional Decision Making* (U.S. Department of Education Institute of Education Sciences National Center for Education Evaluation and Regional Assistance, 2009) at ies.ed.gov/ncee/wwc/pdf/practice_guides/dddm_pg_092909.pdf for various examples of how case study schools found structured time for data use. Also become well versed in how to best implement professional learning communities (PLCs), which can be instrumental in maximizing time spent on data. Then work with your team to establish an approach that works best for your site.

Be a Strong Data Leader

While there is a learning curve to honor for your staff, as an educator leader you will be expected to stay ahead of this curve. Your staff needs to feel confident that you know what you're doing when leading them in data endeavors, and this will help them feel comfortable with data processes. Your staff needs to see you modeling good data use, modeling use of a common (site-wide) data language, and attending their data discussions. Your staff needs to be able to trust that data use is here to stay and not another "adopt and drop" instructional fad. Your staff needs a strong data leader.

Remain aware of the answers to these questions:

- What are my staff's data needs?
- What will my staff's maturing data needs soon be?

The answers can be different for different groups of teachers. For example, the Science Department might be struggling with instructional pacing and need assistance acquiring quality data to analyze, whereas the History Department might already have implemented quality school-wide assessments and need help developing rubrics for more advanced data collection.

Seeing to staff's needs also means spotting and taking care of any major obstacles from the onset of data endeavors. For example, if you have very poor quality (and thus unusable) data due to poor data entry practices, or your data system does not provide every educator with access to its data, or you have multiple data systems with no easy interoperability . . . these are all major issues that will cripple an otherwise well-executed data plan. Start tackling any major issues first to at least get the ball rolling on their improvement.

In a report from the Council of the Great City Schools and the American Institutes for Research, Faria et al. (2012) summarize research concerning how leaders can positively impact data use in school districts, schools, and classrooms. Examples include:

- Clearly articulate expectations and goals.
- Have a clear data use strategy or plan that involves staff buy-in and accountability (e.g., data use is an expected part of one's job).
- Facilitate data use dialogue and collaboration between different levels of leadership and be available for conversations about data.
- Provide high-quality, easy-to-use data and reports (see the "Tools" section of this book).
- Provide useful training, guidance, and coaching activities (see the next "Data Users" chapter).

Faria et al. (2012) also provide a survey distributed to staff and used to assess data use leadership. It is worth reviewing when developing a survey to send your own staff. The more aware you remain of your staff's needs, the better you can lead them.

In addition to meeting staff's needs, a strong data leader also meets students' needs. This involves providing students with regular access to their own data and the support to understand and benefit from this access. For example, your data system should provide student data reports that present the student's own data with student-friendly language. A student portal (often paired with the online data system) where students can regularly log in to access their individual data is important, as is a parent portal (if the two portals are not one and the same) where parents can view their children's data to provide added support. As a leader, ensure students and parents are aware of these resources and know how to use them.

Test Conservatively

Meeting students' needs also involves sparing students from data practices that do not directly support learning and growth. This involves testing conservatively. There are many outspoken opponents of testing, who argue no standardized tests should be given in schools. However, that argument is akin to banning food simply because some people eat to excess and suffer the consequences. Like food, standardized testing has many benefits and is an essential component to well-being: in this case, the well-being of a district's students. However, opponents of standardized testing make some valid points that should be contemplated, and are reactions against the many bad testing practices in place.

Over-testing students, administering poorly crafted tests, and administering tests that render data no one uses are all serious problems that need to be eradicated. Carefully review your department's, school's, or district's annual testing plan, considering all the time that students in each grade level spend testing. Do not overlook:

- national tests like NAEP taken by different grade levels and schools each year;
- state-mandated tests;

- college-related tests like AP, IB, SAT, etc.;
- entrance and exit exams like GATE, Honors, high school graduation, etc.;
- district-mandated tests;
- school-mandated tests;
- tests specific to ELs; etc.

While reviewing your testing plan, consider if any of the following problems are hindering students and/or staff:

- Some populations are tested too heavily (even if testing is not excessive for the site as a whole).
- A type of test that is not state-mandated takes too much testing time.
- The benefits of using data from a particular local test are not enough to warrant its administration.
- The local test is of poor quality.
- The local test is not properly aligned with instruction and/or what we need to know about students.
- The local test is redundant.
- We would be better served by replacing the local test with formative and/or more informal assessment.
- We rely too much on summatively used assessment and not enough on formative assessment.

"Too much" is a subjective phrase, but the precise definition of what constitutes too much testing is hotly debated. I thus leave it up to you to determine what is best for your students and staff, based on feedback you gather. Also, a distinction is drawn between state-mandated tests and local tests, with local tests being those you more likely have the power to change. However, it is still worth contacting state department of education officials regarding problems with mandated tests that are beyond your control. Share the specific problems you identify and ask such officials to review the Council of Chief State School Officers' (2015) framework for ensuring quality state assessments, available at www.ccsso.org/Resources/Publications/Comprehensive_Statewide_Assessment_Systems_A_Framework _for_the_Role_of_the_State_Education_Agency_in_Improving_Quality_and_ Reducing_Burden.html. While awaiting change, however, do what you can to improve administration of your own local assessments.

References

Aladjem, D. K., LeFloch, K. C., Zhang, Y., Kurki, A., Boyle, A., Taylor, J. E., Hermann, S., Uekawa, K., Thomsen, K., & Fashola, O. (2006). *Models matter—The final report of the National Longitudinal Evaluation of Comprehensive School Reform.* Washington, DC: American Institutes for Research (ERIC Document Reproduction Service No. ED499198).

American Statistical Association. (2014, April 8). *ASA statement on using value-added models for educational assessment.* Retrieved from www.amstat.org/policy/pdfs/ASA_VAM_Statement.pdf

Anderegg, C. C. (2007). Classrooms and schools analyzing student data: A study of educational practice. (Doctoral dissertation, Pepperdine University, 2007). *Dissertation Abstracts International, 68*(02A), 184–538.

Bigger, S. L. (2006). Data-driven decision-making within a professional learning community: Assessing the predictive qualities of curriculum-based measurements to a high-stakes, state test of reading achievement at the elementary level. Unpublished doctoral dissertation, University of Pennsylvania, Philadelphia, PA.

Council of Chief State School Officers. (2015). *Comprehensive statewide assessment systems: A framework for the role of the state education agency in improving quality and reducing burden.* Washington, DC: Council of Chief State School Officers. Retrieved from www.ccsso.org/Resources/Publications/Comprehensive_Statewide_Assessment_Systems_A_Framework_for_the_Role_of_the_State_Education_Agency_in_Improving_Quality_and_Reducing_Burden.html

Datnow, A., Park, V., & Wohlstetter, P. (2007). *Achieving with data: How high-performing school systems use data to improve instruction for elementary students.* Los Angeles, CA: University of Southern California, Rossier School of Education, Center on Educational Governance.

Faria, A., Heppen, J., Li, Y., Stachel, S., Jones, W., Sawyer, K., Thomsen, K., Kutner, M., Miser, D., Lewis, S., Casserly, M., Simon, C., Uzzell, R.,

Corcoran, A., & Palacios, M. (2012, Summer). *Charting success: Data use and student achievement in urban schools.* Council of the Great City Schools and the American Institutes for Research. Retrieved from www.cgcs.org/cms/lib/DC00001581/Centricity/Domain/87/Charting_Success.pdf.

Ingram, D., Louis, K. S., & Schroeder, R. G. (2004). Accountability policies and teacher decision making: Barriers to the use of data to improve practice. *Teachers College Record, 106*(6), 1258–1287.

Kotter, J. P. (1996). *Leading change.* Boston, MA: Harvard Business School Press.

Marsh, J. A., Pane, J. F., & Hamilton, L. S. (2006). *Making sense of data-driven decision making in education: Evidence from recent RAND research.* Santa Monica, CA: RAND Corporation.

Rennie Center for Education Research and Policy. (2006, February). *Data-driven teaching: Tools and trends.* Cambridge, MA: Rennie Center for Education Research and Policy.

Song, J., & Felch, J. (2011, April 12). L.A. Unified releases school ratings using "value-added" method. *Los Angeles Times.* Retrieved from www.latimes.com/local/la-me-0413-value-add-20110414-story.html

U.S. Department of Education Institute of Education Sciences (IES) National Center for Education Evaluation (NCEE) and Regional Assistance. (2009). *Using student achievement data to support instructional decision making.* Washington, DC: Author. (ERIC Document Reproduction Service No. ED506645).

Wayman, J. C., & Stringfield, S. (2006). Technology-supported involvement of entire faculties in examination of student data for instructional improvement. *American Journal of Education, 112*(4), 549–571.

Wayman, J. C., Cho, V., & Johnston, M. T. (2007). *The data-informed district: A district-wide evaluation of data use in the Natrona County School District.* Austin, TX: The University of Texas.

Wayman, J. C., Cho, V., & Shaw, S. (2009, December). *First-year results from an efficacy study of the Acuity data system.* Paper presented at the Twenty-fourth Annual Texas Assessment Conference, Austin, TX.

Wohlstetter, P., Datnow, A., & Park, V. (2008). Creating a system for data-driven decision-making: Applying the principal–agent framework. *School Effectiveness and School Improvement, 19*(3), 239–259.

PART IV

Data Users

> What do we live for, if not to
> make life less difficult for each other?
> —Mary Ann Evans (George Eliot)

Who Are Data Users?

Of course, the data users themselves (teachers, administrators, office staff, counselors, etc.) are a primary piece in the puzzle of successful data use. So primary, in fact, that too often they are treated as the *only* piece in data use, with data improvement efforts being focused entirely on professional development (PD) and support staff (e.g., data coaches). PD and support staff can only flourish when effective tools and climate (both covered earlier) are also provided to staff to carry some of the data improvement weight. Without forgetting the importance of good tools and climate, apply this part's and the next chapter's tips to your other efforts to help staff improve data use.

Evaluate Your Data User Support

Evaluating your district's, site's, or group's data user needs and support can help you plan appropriate steps to facilitate any necessary improvements. Online resources can assist your evaluation. These options are available online, so you can choose the format(s) you prefer:

> ### *Time-Saving Resource*
>
> Use these tools in whichever format you prefer (online survey vs. Word document):
>
> - Educational Leader's Evaluation of Site's Data Users' (i.e., Staff's) Needs
> - Staff's Evaluation of Site's Data Users' Needs

- **Online data user needs evaluation (in survey format) that you can complete** to receive results (and an evaluation score) automatically emailed to you.
- **Online data user needs evaluation (in survey format) that staff can complete** to enhance your understanding of staff perception; when staff completes this evaluation using your email address, results (and an evaluation score) will be automatically emailed to you every time another staff member completes the form; a better option is to copy/paste these evaluation questions into a new, single survey form you manage (using a tool like Google Doc Forms or SurveyMonkey) so all staff members' responses can be easily aggregated.
- **Word file of data user needs evaluation (which you can edit as necessary to suit your site) you can complete** on your computer or in printed form to evaluate your site's data user needs and support while also adding notes concerning steps you plan to take to improve areas (which the next chapter will help you determine).
- **Word file of data user needs evaluation (which you can edit as necessary to suit your site) staff can complete** to enhance your

understanding of staff perception; staff can complete this in hard copy format, or you can copy/paste these evaluation questions into a new, single survey form you manage so all staff members' responses can be easily aggregated.

While completing the evaluation, refer to this book as necessary (particularly the next chapter) to better understand any of the evaluation's questions.

Use the evaluation in whatever way is most helpful for you. For example, you and your colleagues might discuss and complete the evaluation as a district department, or you might reflect on all of the evaluation's questions by yourself and write notes beside each question.

See the "Evaluate Your Data Use Climate" section for additional guidelines that are also applicable when evaluating data user support. You can return to this survey as often as you like to reevaluate your support of staff over time.

10 | Data User Maximization

How to Empower Data Users

All staff members using data within a school or school district need to be empowered and supported in using that data correctly, easily, and for most cases in which data can be an asset. Improving how staff uses data is an ongoing, multifaceted process. This chapter contains strategies most important to that process, as well as strategies most frequently neglected by

> ### Checklist for Improving Staff Data Skills
>
> - Ongoing, embedded PD
> - Capitalize on the range of PD formats
> - Differentiate PD
> - Use real data during PD
> - Provide tools to apply—rather than memorize—good data practices
> - Employ the good instructional strategies you expect teachers to model
> - Embrace learning curves and implementation order
> - Establish norms for collaborative time
> - Establish straightforward goals for collaborative time
> - Find and prepare support staff.

educator leaders. By employing each of these strategies (and/or advocating for leaders above you to apply them), you can maximize your data users' chances of making data work for them and the students they serve.

Ongoing, Embedded PD

Research contains evidence on the limitations of short-term training models (e.g., common, single-instance workshops). This "drive-by" PD, rampant in U.S. school districts, has little effect on educator practice and virtually zero effect on student achievement (Darling-Hammond & Falk, 2013). In order for PD to have an impact on practice, it cannot be structured to be forgotten. Rather, PD must:

- illustrate specifically how the learned concept will "look" in real-world practice;
- integrate with other educational endeavors to mirror real-world implementation (e.g., talk about acquiring informal, formative assessment during instructional strategy training since one endeavor is a natural piece of the other);
- be paired with follow-up and accountability (e.g., an administrator attends PLC data dialogues to see the concept being applied, an instructional coach visits classrooms to see the data-informed lessons in action, etc.);
- be ongoing (the next section will provide format ideas, and the "Give the Gift of Time" section in Chapter 9, "How to Maximize Climate", offers help with finding time).

Capitalize on the Range of PD Formats

It is easier to provide ongoing PD when you recognize the varied formats through which staff can learn about data use:

- **traditional** training sessions, workshops, or in-services;
- **PLCs**, which can go by many names;

- **classroom visitations**, sometimes in the form of "walk-throughs"; these can be teachers observing peers or can involve consultants or administrators;
- **mentorship** or professional partnering;
- **co-teaching**, which does not have to be formally scheduled; rather, teachers can come together to co-teach particular lessons (e.g., those added to the LMS based on data-indicated success) or to group students (with each teacher's group addressing different student needs);
- **certificate-earning**: the National Board for Professional Teaching Standards (NBPTS) certification requires educators to spend considerable time analyzing and reflecting on their instructional practice, which involves data;
- **continuing education**: local universities sometimes offer arrangements where a group of staff members can complete a program together at a reduced cost;
- **online courses**: University of California, Berkeley (UCB) has a Master's in Data Science program that is taught entirely online (requestinfo.datascience.berkeley.edu), and there are hundreds of massive open online courses (MOOCs) that can be taken for free;
- **webinars** or online seminars: for example, All Analytics (www.allanalytics.com) hosts free, ongoing webinars that often relate to education data;
- **in-person conferences**: I have found the most prestigious (and most focused on education data) to be the STATS-DC Conference put on by the National Center for Education Statistics (NCES), within the U.S. Department of Education's Institute of Education Sciences (IES);
- **online conferences**: there are many free, quality conferences online that often offer data-related sessions (you can check schedules ahead of time); examples include the K-12 Online Conference and a number of conferences organized annually by Steve Hargadon: the Global Education Conference, Library 2.0, the School Leadership Summit, OZeLIVE! (Australia's Edtech Conference), and others are all listed at his event and newsletter website (www.LearningRevolution.com);
- **district-wide staff development event**: before you think, "Oh, you mean just a regular training day," consider a district event that has a

conference feel; leverage your own colleagues' data talent to present in different classrooms and let staff members attend the sessions that most relate to their needs; try to get your DSRP to hold sessions in other classrooms, as well, and arrange for a phenomenal keynote speaker to set an excited tone for data use;

- **"unconferences"** and EdCamps: your site can even organize its own;
- **professional learning networks (PLNs)** involve using various tools (e.g., social media) to connect with colleagues for flexible learning;
- **Twitter**: I resisted opening a Twitter account for years until a colleague convinced me of its PD value; now much of the new data-related studies and literature I learn of is due to tweets (I repost the best ones at @OTCData); encourage staff to run Twitter searches for #eddata, #datause, and #assessment to learn from a host of current sources;
- **contests** that engage staff in supplementary data-related tasks;
- **action research** participation;
- **Connected Educators**: visit connectededucators.org for a free Connected Educator Starter Kit (this provides an invaluable introduction to various avenues for professional collaboration and learning).

More examples abound. Engaging staff in varied PD formats empowers staff members to choose and utilize PD that works best for them. Exposing each staff member to multiple PD formats also prevents PD from getting stale. As you seek out, discover, and share varied sources of data use PD with staff, it also helps staff to view you as a strong data leader who keeps abreast of the latest data use research.

Differentiate PD

Note how varied PD options make it easier to differentiate PD for staff based on their learning preferences, schedules, and needs. Different staff members will commonly be at different stages of data use competency.

When you periodically survey staff to assess areas with which they need help, as well as their most desired venues for learning, you can provide targeted PD most likely to facilitate growth. SurveyMonkey (www.surveymonkey.com) and Google Forms (www.google.com/forms/) offer easy ways to survey staff and are not difficult for most users to learn to use. These free surveying options will require minimal time compared to hard-copy or email approaches. Be sure your surveys are clear, to the point, and short (e.g., ten questions at most).

Post-PD surveys can also help you understand what worked, what did not work, and what is still needed. Sharing survey results with teachers provides transparency concerning PD's successes and failures, and provides incentive for teachers to offer thoughtful feedback (Hess, 2015).

A fundamental guideline for all assessments of staff's PD needs is that what you learn is reflected in future PD and related supports. In other words, if you learn your staff doesn't get much from five-minute data segments at staff meetings, cut or revamp those segments.

Providing a variety of PD options to staff learning to use data is important in the same way differentiating learning opportunities for students is important. Differentiation gives each learner a better chance to grow.

Use Real Data During PD

When staff members learn to use data while looking at data that is fictional or not related to them, they are less engaged in the learning process. When staff members learn to use a data system to generate reports of data that is fictional or not related to them, they are less engaged in the learning process. In either case, they are less likely to walk away from the training with these wins:

- "After looking at *my* data with guidance, I can already make a data-informed decision that will help students."
- "I know I can apply the learned data use concepts to *my* own data, because I just did it! I'm far less nervous to do it on my own now."
- "After viewing *my* data during the data system training, I can already make a data-informed decision that will help students."
- "I know I can use the data system to analyze *my* own data, because I just did it! I'm far less nervous to use the data system on my own now."

When planning training on the use of data or a data system, take steps to ensure participants will each have access to their own timely data, just as they will when applying learned concepts after the training, on their own.

Provide Tools to Apply—Rather Than Memorize—Good Data Practices

Do you remember your university Statistics class? Math majors are the only ones I have ever seen smile at the recollection. If you train staff on all the best practices of data use, their heads will likely be spinning afterwards. Arm educators with a reference tool that summarizes the main points they will need to apply when using data. It should trigger prior learning rather than go into depth. An example is provided for you here and the online version can be customized.

> ### *Time-Saving Resource*
>
> Use the electronic version of the following page, which you can type within and/or manipulate to customize for your staff.

I am not talking about a massive binder; I am talking about a one-page reference sheet. A notation should be included on the sheet that directs staff to a resource (e.g., a URL for the data system's help lesson covering each data use concept) and a person (e.g., a name and contact information for the site's data coach) from which staff can acquire additional help for data and data system use.

To better understand what data knowledge and skills staff should possess, refer to *SLDS Data Use Standards: Knowledge, Skills, and Professional Behaviors for Effective Data Use* (see Statewide Longitudinal Data Systems Grant Program, 2015), which is available at www.slds.grads360.org/#communities/pdc/documents/5204. These standards serve as a comprehensive resource in many other areas of data use, as well, and are worth examining.

Data Users

 Sample Data Use Reference Tool You Can Modify

Data Use Reference

Analyze data to **investigate** a question, theory, hunch, or finding; ask:

- Have **all factors** been explored (e.g., relevant data, multiple sources of feedback, etc.)?
- Am I sure the problem is **a problem** (statistical significance, reliability, sample size, etc.)?
- Have I **pinpointed** where the problem is (previous grade, only some courses, really a reading comprehension issue, etc.)?

Impact on Data?

Assessment Quality

Instruction

Curriculum

Instructional Pacing

Resources

Program

Classroom Management

Outside Curriculum (e.g., student organizational skills)

Organizational Structure (schedule, calendar, etc.)

Professional Development

Support (mentorship, PLC, etc.)

Stakeholder Involvement

School Culture

Common Language

Authentic Assessment = students do real-world tasks to demonstrate mastery

Disaggregate = break data into smaller groups

Formative = use the assessment to guide current practice/instruction

Measure = a way to judge something like learning

Qualitative Data = subjective & often text-based, like writing rubric scores

Quantitative Data = objective & #-based, like multiple choice test scores

Rubric = a scoring tool/grid with incremental criteria that is often categorized

Standards = what we teach (like CCSS & NGSS)

Subgroup = a student group type like race/ethnicity, EL, gender, socioeconomically disadvantaged, or students with disabilities

Summative = use the assessment to judge past practice/instruction

Don't Forget:

Correlation (*A* & *B* happened) doesn't always = causation (*A* caused *B*)

Use **multiple measures** (not 1 test) to guide conclusions

Use **varied measures** (not all tests) to guide conclusions

At least 10 kids in **sample** before generalization

A **trend** = at least 3 years

Disaggregate data to check on subgroups, not just all students

Data Help = www.[URL].com or Noah D. Data 888-8888 Noah@district.com

Data System Help = www.[URL].com or Syd Stem 999-9999 syd@tech.com

Experience from the Field

"In July 2012, I was hired as a Business Intelligence Coordinator to create a systemic PD system around data use. While MNPS did have district data coaches, there were only 12 for the 150 schools that we have. Therefore, we needed to think 'outside the box' to provide data use supports in a timely manner to educators.

After conducting a needs assignment, I developed the Data-Informed Decision Making Ecosystem (see diagram). PD does not happen in isolation, and several supports need to be in place at one time to provide a balanced PD approach for building educators' capacity to use data for making informed decisions for increasing student achievement.

Using Race to the Top funding, MNPS had addressed data access and was providing some data literacy and analysis support through data coaches. By implementing OTCD standards within the data system, a common language for the data was created and documented in data guides. The data guides were useful in providing just in time PD support to educators throughout the district."

—Dr. Margie L. Johnson, Business Intelligence Coordinator
Metropolitan Nashville Public Schools

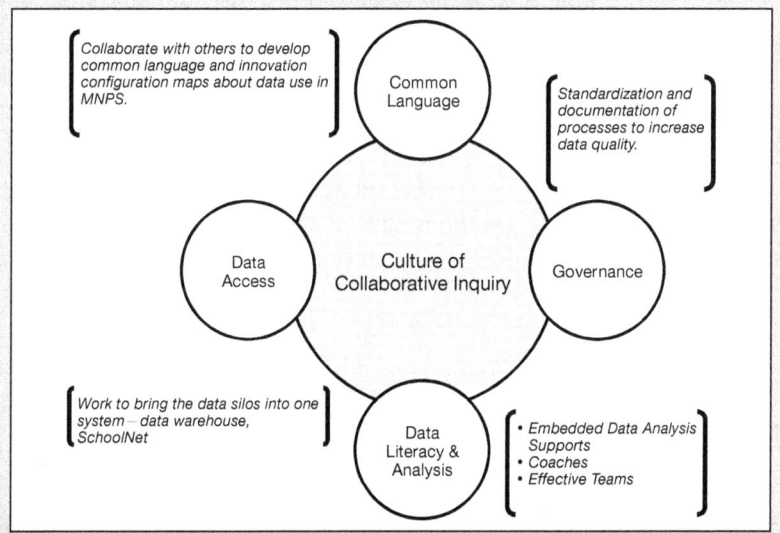

Figure 10.1 Data-Informed Decision Making Ecosystem

Employ the Good Instructional Strategies You Expect Teachers to Model

I attended a fantastic in-service on promoting student engagement in which the facilitators modeled the same kind of instructional strategies they were teaching participants to use. It made for a more engaging event, we got to see the recommended strategies in action, and we walked away with the increased likelihood of utilizing the strategies well, as we better understood how to do so.

Even if the main topic of your PD event is data or data-related technology, the facilitator should still be modeling the various instructional strategies we know to be *good teaching*. These strategies work for student learners, and they also work (modified for age-appropriateness when necessary) for adult learners.

Embrace Learning Curves and Implementation Order

A site's data use is an evolving process. Establishing a sense of urgency is vital to launching school-wide or district-wide change. However, be prepared to progress from light to deep understanding of good data practices. For example, if you direct staff to discuss student performance on assessment questions without first establishing a common language to use, or without teaching staff how to assess students' thinking by the distractors (i.e., wrong answers) they select, the discussions will prove ineffective.

Embracing gradual steps also relates to your site's data culture continuum. For example, on the road to data-informed improvement and transparency, you can expect your staff to pass through these stages:

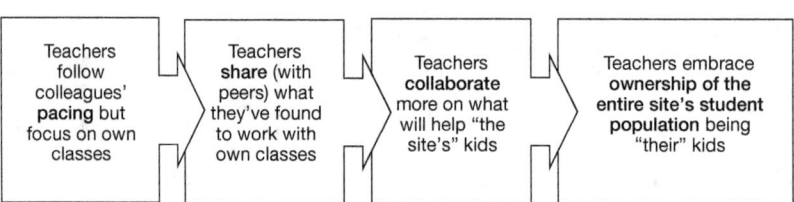

Figure 10.2

You should also honor your site's readiness for related implementations. For example, do not make major decisions based on data from assessments known to be poor. Rather, rework those assessments first while using data that is more respected.

A good rule of practice is to consider the timeline for any data-related endeavor. For example, if you want to implement standardized assessments for use on a formative basis (i.e., realizing that *informal* assessment of students for daily formative feedback is a separate matter), you generally need to implement components in this order:

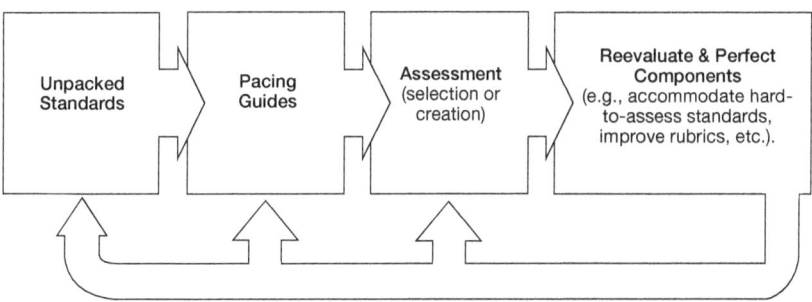

Figure 10.3

Whatever your data endeavor, determine where your staff and site land on the diagram. Next, determine the stages through which your staff will likely pass on the road to your endeavor's accomplishment, as well as the stages through which your implementation needs to pass. This way you can plan to offer staff the support they need at each stage, and you can offer them implementation stages that will best pave the way for your ultimate data goals.

Note staff groups might be in different stages at different times. This chapter's section on "Differentiate PD" can help.

Establish Norms for Collaborative Time

Each PLC or other collaborative group should develop norms that will help them make the most of their time together. You might offer norm suggestions, but the ultimate verbiage should be selected by the team with each member's buy-in. Examples of norms include:

- Be on time and leave on time;
- Everyone talks equally (if you're shy, lean in, if you're outspoken, rein it in);
- Any electronic devices are used for tasks (no checking email or working on unrelated work);
- Show respect for people and their ideas.

Notice these norms are few and succinct. A group's norms should be visible at each of the group's meetings.

Establish Straightforward Goals for Collaborative Time

When staff gets together on a particular day to work with data, the goals for their meeting might be as simple as:

1. **How did I do?** Use the data system's *Multi-Measure Report* to determine which CCSSs from the last unit represent strengths and which represent weaknesses for your own class(es). Consider:
   - how your class performed on one CCSS versus the other.
   - how your scores compare to school-wide averages.
2. **What help will I acquire?** Identify a colleague who had success on a CCSS with which your students struggled and ask that he or she describe the likely cause and add the resource to the district's LMS within three days. If your struggle was a school-wide struggle, discuss where your group will acquire assistance.
3. **What help will I share?** Identify the likely cause of any successes (CCSSs for which you significantly exceeded school-wide averages) and briefly describe it for your colleagues (while letting them know you will add this resource to the district's LMS within three days). If your success was a school-wide success, discuss the likely cause and who will add relevant resources to the LMS within three days.

As time advances and so does your staff's data use, you can move on to more advanced goals, such as determining if any subgroup gaps have significantly widened or narrowed in particular areas. However, start with goals comparable to each group's data competence so goals can be accomplished and the time beneficial.

Remember: you do not only want time for the data to be analyzed—you also want time for staff to (or at least begin to) devise a data-informed action. Highly effective data reports (obtained by following the "Tools" section of this book) will make data analyses faster and more successful. This will provide more time for groups to fully accomplish established goals.

Find and Prepare Support Staff

If you can secure funds for qualified support staff (e.g., site data coaches, district instructional coaches, grade/department chairs, technology coordinator, etc.), the more the better. Educators should improve data analysis accuracy through the use of staff such as leaders, data teams, and/or instructional coaches (Bennett & Gitomer, 2009; Cho & Wayman, 2009; Knapp, Swinnerton, Copland, & Monpas-Hubar, 2006; Marsh et al., 2006; McLaughlin & Talbert, 2006; National Forum on Education Statistics, 2011; Supovitz & Klein, 2003; USDEOPEPD, 2009; VanWinkle et al., 2011; Wayman, 2005; Wayman, Snodgrass Rangel, Jimerson, & Cho, 2010). At the very least, identify teacher leaders and designate a willing educator as the "go to" person for data use support and the "go to" person for data system (i.e., technology) support.

However, do not just assume these helpers automatically have the skills needed to be staff's "go to" people. This is especially true as staff's data skills advance or as new technology (e.g., data systems, technology that integrates with a data system, etc.) is introduced. Rather, provide support staff with the PD and collaborative time required to enable them to remain an asset to the rest of the team. This will enable support staff to continually nurture and grow site-wide expertise.

References

Bennett, R. E., & Gitomer, D. H. (2009). Transforming K-12 assessment: Integrating accountability testing, formative assessment and professional support. In C. Wyatt-Smith & J. J. Cumming (Eds.), *Educational assessment in the 21st century*, 43–61. New York, NY: Springer.

Cho, V., & Wayman, J. C. (2009, April). *Knowledge management and educational data use*. Paper presented at the 2009 Annual Meeting of the American Educational Research Association, San Diego, CA.

Darling-Hammond, L., & Falk, B. (2013, September 12). Teacher learning through assessment: How student-performance assessments can support teacher learning. Center for American Progress. Retrieved from www.americanprogress.org/issues/education/report/2013/09/12/73978/teacher-learning-through-assessment/

Hess, F. M. (2015, April). Speaking up for better schools. *Education Week, 72*(7). Alexandria, VA: ASCD.

Knapp, M. S., Swinnerton, J. A., Copland, M. A., & Monpas-Hubar, J. (2006). *Data-informed leadership in education*. Seattle, WA: Center for the Study of Teaching and Policy.

McLaughlin, M., & Talbert, J. E. (2006). *Building school-based teacher learning communities: Professional strategies to improve student achievement*. New York, NY: Teachers College Press.

Marsh, J. A., Pane, J. F., & Hamilton, L. S. (2006). *Making sense of data-driven decision making in education: Evidence from recent RAND research*. Santa Monica, CA: RAND Corporation.

National Forum on Education Statistics. (2011). *Traveling through time: The forum guide to longitudinal data systems. Book Four of Four: Advanced LDS Usage* (NFES 2011–802). Washington, DC: National Center for Education Statistics, Institute of Education Sciences, U.S. Department of Education.

Statewide Longitudinal Data Systems Grant Program. (2015). *SLDS Data Use Standards: Knowledge, Skills, and Professional Behaviors for Effective Data Use, Version 2*. U.S. Department of Education. Washington, DC: National Center for Education Statistics.

Supovitz, J. A., & Klein, V. (2003). *Mapping a course for improved student learning: How innovative schools systematically use student performance data to guide improvement.* Philadelphia, PA: Consortium for Policy Research in Education.

U.S. Department of Education Office of Planning, Evaluation and Policy Development. (2009). *Implementing data-informed decision making in schools: Teacher access, supports and use.* United States Department of Education (ERIC Document Reproduction Service No. ED504191).

VanWinkle, W., Vezzu, M., & Zapata-Rivera, D. (2011). Question-based reports for policymakers. *ETS Research Memorandum. RM-11–16.* Princeton, NJ: ETS.

Wayman, J. C. (2005). Involving teachers in data-driven decision making: Using computer data systems to support teacher inquiry and reflection. *Journal of Education for Students Placed At Risk, 10*(3), 295–308.

Wayman, J. C., Snodgrass Rangel, V. W., Jimerson, J. B., & Cho, V. (2010). *Improving data use in NISD: Becoming a data-informed district.* Austin, TX: The University of Texas at Austin.

PART

Conclusion

Optimism is the faith that leads to achievement.
Nothing can be done without hope and confidence.
—Helen Keller

Put It All Together

Where to Begin

After completing each section's evaluations (described below), you should have a clear idea of the areas in which your tools, climate, or staff supports are struggling. Use this information to develop an action plan that details how you and your team will generate any necessary improvements.

> ### Time-Saving Resource
>
> Use any evaluations described in this book, using whichever format you prefer (online survey vs. Word document), to examine your tools, climate, and data user support. You will find the following types of evaluations for each of those three areas:
>
> - Educational Leader's Evaluation
> - Staff's Evaluation
>
> The Word versions of these forms can also be used to record action plans.

The evaluation forms provided in Word format can be used to record your action plans for tools, climate, and data users. Good action plans address detail-related questions like *Who will do this? When will this be done? How will we measure improvement?* etc. However, the forms have been kept simple so as to not encumber you. Thus you can use or modify them to fit other plan formats (like an action plan format you are required to use for accountability compliance). You are welcome to add specific details as you go, or to use the forms as brainstorming tools and then develop a more detailed action plan afterwards.

Regardless of your approach, the goal is to engage in honest reflection and to develop relevant steps you and your team will put into action. Refer to relevant sections of the book to inform the steps you plan to take.

Real-World Implementation

It can help to learn from a real-world implementation. Dr. Margie Johnson is the Business Intelligence Coordinator at Metropolitan Nashville Public Schools (MNPS) in Tennessee. Dr. Johnson has successfully implemented reference guides, which the district calls *data guides*, and other OTCD Standards at MNPS. In the following interview, Dr. Johnson tells of her experience embedding data guides in the nationally recognized data warehouse that MNPS built.

Q1: Please give us some background on your district. For example, how is it that you have control over your own data warehouse?

A1: MNPS serves over 81,000 students at 153 different schools covering pre-Kindergarten through adult classes. Approximately 80 percent of our students participate in Free and Reduced Lunch and 20 percent are LEP. There are over 6,500 certificated MNPS staff members. We used Race to the Top to hire programmers to build our data warehouse. We used the OtisEd framework and built it on Microsoft.

Q2: How did you go about designing your data guides, such as determining the format and what types of information to include?

A2: The data guides are based off of Dr. Jenny Rankin's work (OTCD). I adapted them a bit for our needs, such as changing the name to *data guide*. I also used sections from her samples. All information on the data guides is gathered through a collaborative process. I start by creating a draft, and then I invite the necessary parties to a meeting to discuss the data guide and what needs to be in the guide.

Q3: **Once you determined your data guides' format, who created each data guide? For example, did you create them all yourself or did you involve a team in the process?**

A3: I create the rough draft, but meet with the department(s) that uses the data the most and ask them to review and for input about the message they want conveyed throughout the district. The next draft is reviewed by the department and the data warehouse team before being disseminated.

Q4: **How do users go about accessing the data guides when they are using the data warehouse?**

A4: Each data guide is linked to its respective report.

Q5: **What are some ways you let staff know the data guides are available to help them use data?**

A5: The *MNPS Data Spotlight Newsletter* spotlights exemplary data use throughout the district and the latest data guide available. We also have the information on our Intranet site.

Q6: **What feedback have you gotten from your staff about the data guides, and how are the data guides supporting your staff's data understanding and use?**

A6: I use URL shorteners to track the number of views. The feedback from meeting with central office teams has been positive, as the data guide has facilitated us creating a common language about the data. It's helping build capacity throughout the district to ensure that the data is used appropriately to make informed decisions about increasing student achievement.

Q7: **Did you encounter any obstacles when implementing the data guides? If so, how did you overcome these obstacles?**

A7: One issue we have had is linking the guides in our data system and being able to track usage. We are hoping the URL shortener helps. The other issue is making sure users see the data guide. Right now, they are part of the header and sometimes get lost on the page. However, the other principles of OTCD have helped, particularly with labeling and header/footers for each report.

Conclusion

Dr. Johnson is also renowned for her professional development, data use climate, and other efforts to support staff in effective data use. She understands how all the pieces come together to support staff in a variety of ways. As Dr. Johnson found, OTCD principles help other efforts to improve data use. For example, one set of OTCD Standards can help *another* set of OTCD Standards be more successful, and the same is true of efforts promoting effective climate and data users.

Thus as you implement more standards over time, you will often find even more success with those already implemented. I am grateful to Dr. Johnson for this valuable insight into real-world implementation. Many others—including educators and commercial DSRPs—are also finding success in implementing concepts covered in this book. Pick an area to start with, and see what happens.

Final Words

Imagine data that is easy for educators to understand and use, because:

- the data tools being used to view data adhere to best practices for reporting data to educators (i.e., data is "over-the-counter" and thus easy to understand and use);
- the data use climate supports and inspires staff; and
- data users have the ongoing professional development and guidance they need.

Now imagine an environment that does not offer such assistance. Think of the impact this book's concepts have on data-using educators and—most importantly—students. Remember research indicating that most educators are analyzing data incorrectly in typical data use environments (which do not adhere to a majority of this book's standards).

As you take steps outlined in this book, encourage dialogue about making data work for educators. Share this book with others in the education, edtech, and research communities and discuss its implications as new developments in these communities arise. Remember:

- Less than half of educators' data analyses (using typical, hard-to-understand reports) are accurate, despite the benefits of traditional interventions like PD and staffing-based supports.
- Educators constitute a favorable user base largely not to blame for most poor data use.
- Educators' data misunderstandings directly impact students.
- Making data work for educators by following standards in this book has been shown to improve educators' data analyses by up to 436 percent (Rankin, 2013).

As educators, we are entrusted with the care of kids' lives. Students are at our mercy and it is our job to do the best we can to help them. If you are an educator, I assume you share this goal. If you are an educator who shares data with others, I imagine you cannot decline this chance to see gains like 436 percent that ultimately affect students. I know you can use this book to make data work for your colleagues and other stakeholders, and I trust that you will. Thank you for going the extra mile to help students and the educators who teach and nurture them.

Reference

Rankin, J. G. (2013). *Over-the-counter data's impact on educators' data analysis accuracy.* ProQuest Dissertations and Theses, 3575082. Retrieved from pqdtopen.proquest.com/doc/1459258514.html?FMT=ABS

PART

Appendix

Data system and report providers need to make data "over-the-counter"—and thus easy to understand and use—by following the research-based standards on the upcoming pages. These standards concern reporting the data effectively and with embedded usage support. *Designing Data Reports that Work: A Guide for Creating Data Systems in Schools and Districts*, another book by Dr. Jenny Grant Rankin, explains how to best implement each standard.

Appendix

 Over-the-Counter Data (OTCD) Standards

LABEL

Just like over-the-counter medication, data needs to be properly labeled to ensure it is used easily and appropriately. *Label* standards are organized by *Titles* and *Footers*.

1.1   TITLES

Title refers to the name of a report that communicates education data. The 1.1 standards pertain to title design.

1.1.01 Present

Give each report its own, distinct title that remains consistent between (a) when it is displayed within a **report list** and (b) when it is featured directly on the **report**, in which case it should be prominent at the top of the page.

1.1.02 Communicate What Is Inside the Report

Clearly communicate what type of data the report displays and/or *how* it displays data (e.g., report type). Use a title that functions well both (a) when the report is **closed** and users are determining which report(s) to open/view in the data system, and (b) when the report is **open** (viewed within the data system or printed) and users need a quick indication of its contents.

1.1.03 Use Consistent Titling System

Utilize a consistent titling system within the data system or report suite. E.g., if one report title ends with the word "List" to indicate its format involves listing scores of multiple entities, titles of like reports should also end with "List".

1.1.04 Use Concise Language that Maximizes Info Communicated

Be concise while also communicating the *most pertinent* info a user needs to know when determining if this is the report he or she needs; i.e., do not try to accommodate all of a report's descriptors in its title. Be as concise as good sense allows; e.g., the term "3-Yr" works better than "Multi-Yr" in the title of a report that displays up to three years of data because "3-Yr" communicates more info while also using fewer characters (reducing clutter).

1.1.05 Leave Some Info for the Header and/or Input Controls

Do not cram ancillary info (that can be determined by users' input control selections) into the title. Instead, let users control details like "Students: Asian," "Grouped by: Course," etc. and display these selections *under* the report's title in less prominent font.

1.2   FOOTERS

A footer is an annotation at the bottom of a data report page (though other locations can suffice) that helps the user understand and/or analyze the report's contents. The 1.2 standards pertain to footer design.

1.2.01 Present

Place a report-specific footer (as described in this section) on each data report.

1.2.02 Only Communicate Most Crucial Info

Only include info that is crucial for users to correctly understand and interpret the data. E.g., clearly communicate how users can avoid the mistakes or confusion most commonly experienced when using the report and its data.

1.2.03 Follow Length Guidelines (Short)

Establish and utilize system-wide guidelines concerning footer length that are followed with minimal (if any) exceptions, noting users are likely to ignore lengthy text. E.g., landscape/horizontally orientated reports might have footers of up to 328 characters (including spaces), and portrait/vertically orientated reports might have footers of up to 243 characters (including spaces).

1.2.04 Follow Font Guidelines (Same Size/Type as Report's Data)

Establish and utilize system-wide guidelines requiring the footer's font size to be the same as that used for most data in the report (resist the urge to make the footer smaller). Also use the same font *type* whenever appropriate.

SUPPLEMENTAL DOCUMENTATION

Not all info a user needs to know can fit in the label, so supplemental documentation offers further explanation for the analysis and use of a report's data. *Supplemental Documentation* standards are organized by *Reference Sheets* and *Reference Guides*.

2.1 REFERENCE SHEETS

A reference sheet (often called an abstract) is a single page accompanying a report to help the user more easily understand the report and analyze its data. The 2.1 standards pertain to reference sheet design.

2.1.01 Present

Provide a reference sheet for every report, explaining that specific report. Include the sheet even for simple reports to offer users assurance/consistency.

2.1.02 Accessible

Make the sheet easily accessible with an obvious report-to-sheet **link** and with **PDF** downloading and **printing** capabilities.

2.1.03 Helpful Contents

Include helpful contents like: (a) **title** at the top of the reference sheet matching the title of the report, with the nature of the sheet ("Reference Sheet") underneath; (b) **description** of the sheet's purpose and any abbreviations used; (c) and a reduced **image** of what the report generally looks like when it has been generated (images can be "stacked" to show multiple report pages with significant differences); as well as sections for (d) **"Purpose"** (answering, "What are some questions this report will help answer?"; (e) **"Focus"** answering, "Who is the intended audience?" "What data is reported?" and "How is the data reported?" and (f) **"Warning"** answering, "What do many educators misunderstand?" in a way

Appendix

that helps users overcome mistakes most likely to be made when analyzing this report's data.

2.1.04 Follow Consistency Guidelines

Remain consistent in (a) **appearance** (e.g., order of info, layout, color choices, etc.) and (b) **content** type (e.g., users can expect the same types of info from each reference sheet).

2.2 REFERENCE GUIDES

A reference guide (often called an interpretation guide) is a two- or three-page reference guide that accompanies a report in order to help the educator more easily *use* the report and analyze its data. The 2.2 standards pertain to reference guide design.

2.2.01 Present

Provide a reference guide for every report, explaining that specific report. Include the guide even for simple reports to offer users assurance/consistency.

2.2.02 Accessible

Make the guide easily accessible with an obvious report-to-guide **link** and with **PDF** downloading and **printing** capabilities.

2.2.03 Helpful Contents

Include helpful sections like: (a) **reference sheet** (as described in Standard 2.1.03) as the reference guide's first page, followed by sections for (b) "**Instructions**" answering/illustrating, "How do I read the report?"; (c) "**Essential Questions**" answering/illustrating each question listed under "Purpose: What are some questions . . ." on the guide's first page; and (d) "**More Info**" answering questions that lead users to additional info on related topics.

2.2.04 Follow Consistency Guidelines

Remain consistent in (a) **appearance** (e.g., order of info, layout, color choices, etc.) and (b) **content** type (e.g., users can expect the same types of info from each reference guide).

HELP SYSTEM

An online help system, accessible via link from the data system, contains lessons to help users perform tasks and understand topics. *Help System* standards are organized by *Tech Lessons* and *Data Analysis Lessons*.

3.1 TECH LESSONS (USING THE SYSTEM)

Tech lessons help users to use the data system (e.g., what to click, where to look, etc.), acting like a virtual tech coach/trainer who can assist users when a live person who can help is not present, Customer Support is closed, and/or this training tool is desired. The 3.1 standards pertain to tech lesson design.

3.1.01 Present

Offer a comprehensive set of tech lessons to cover all common technical tasks and key technical topics.

3.1.02 Accessible

Make lessons: (a) accessible **online** (e.g., users can share a lesson's URL with other users, Customer Support can share a lesson's URL with a user asking for help, etc.), (b) logically **organized** so they are easy to manually locate within the help system, (c) **searchable** (e.g., users can enter a term like "generate report" within the help system and links to relevant lessons will appear), (d) with **PDF** downloading and **printing** capabilities, and (e) (in addition to the ever-present help system link) place a specific **lesson link**/button in each pertinent data system area (e.g., in the part of the system where users create custom reports, offer a link directly to the "Create Custom Report" lesson).

3.1.03 Include Lessons for All Users

Include lessons to meet all users' needs, remembering even "intuitive" systems and processes are not intuitive to users lacking tech-familiarity. E.g., some users will need a lesson on how to log into the data system.

3.1.04 Key Features

Make lessons: (a) **task-specific** (e.g., do not cram a single lesson with everything users might want to do in a module), with few **topic-specific** exceptions; (b) **step-by-step** (e.g., "1. Click *Search* in the top-right corner of your screen . . ."); and (c) **illustrated** (e.g., show what the relevant portion of the screen looks like during each lesson segment, with numbers superimposed on the image to match numbered steps explained in the lesson, etc.).

Appendix

3.1.05 Follow Consistency Guidelines

Remain consistent in (a) **appearance** (e.g., order of info, layout, color choices, etc.) and (b) **content** type (e.g., users can expect the same types of info from each of the same types of lessons).

3.2 DATA ANALYSIS LESSONS

Data analysis lessons help users to understand, analyze, and use data in the system (e.g., "Understand State Accountability Measures"), acting like a virtual data coach/trainer who can assist users when a live person who can help is not present, Customer Support is closed, and/or this training tool is desired. The 3.2 standards pertain to data lesson design.

3.2.01 Present

Offer a comprehensive set of data analysis lessons to cover all common data-related tasks and key data-related topics.

3.2.02 Accessible

Make lessons: (a) accessible **online** (e.g., users can share a lesson's URL with other users, Customer Support can share a lesson's URL with a user asking for help, etc.), (b) logically **organized** so they are easy to manually locate within the help system, (c) **searchable** (e.g., users can enter a term like "data dialogues" within the help system and links to relevant lessons will appear), (d) with **PDF** downloading and **printing** capabilities, and (e) (in addition to the ever-present help system link) place a specific **lesson link**/button in each pertinent data system area (e.g., in the part of the system where users customize intervention tiers, offer a link directly to the "Use Intervention Tiers" lesson).

3.2.03 Include Lessons for All Users

Include lessons to meet all users' needs, remembering educators vary greatly in data skills and comfort levels. E.g., some users will need introductory lessons with definitions of common terms.

3.2.04 Key Features

Make lessons: (a) **topic-specific** (e.g., do not cram a single lesson with everything users might want to do with data), with some **task-specific** exceptions (e.g., "Use Results to Differentiate Instruction");

(b) **region-specific** (e.g., as concerns specific assessments and their guidelines); and (c) **illustrated** (e.g., diagrams, classroom layouts, etc.).

3.2.05 Follow Consistency Guidelines

Remain consistent in (a) **appearance** (e.g., order of info, layout, color choices, etc.) and (b) **content** type (e.g., users can expect the same types of info from each of the same types of lessons).

PACKAGE/DISPLAY

The manner in which data is packaged and displayed for users needs to promote easy and accurate understanding/analysis/use of the data. *Package/Display* standards are organized by *Credibility, Key Features, Design, Navigation,* and *Input Controls*.

4.1   CREDIBILITY

A credible data system or report suite is one users can trust as accurate and appropriate. The 4.1 standards pertain to ways data systems and reports must establish and maintain credibility.

4.1.01 No Wrong Data

Safeguard against displaying incorrect data. E.g., ensure: (a) **reports work** properly (e.g., do not "duplicate-count" or erroneously convert a numeric score to a percent); (b) reports pull data from the **right places**; (c) original **data files** are as appropriately formatted, clean/correct, and complete as possible.

4.1.02 No Inappropriate Displays or Calculations

When determining how to display data and how to calculate values: (a) adhere to guidelines **specific to the data** being displayed (e.g., don't show accountability scores over time on a line graph, implying growth, if those particular accountability scores cannot be used to determine growth) or calculated (e.g., do not subtract one grade level's test score from another's and emphasize the difference if that particular test is not scaled across grade levels), (b) select displays and calculations most likely to **encourage correct** analyses of the particular data being displayed, and (c) do **not simplify** the data presentation to the point that misunderstandings are likely.

4.1.03 No Sloppiness

Ensure the data system and its reports contain no: (a) **misspellings**, (b) errors in **grammar** or **capitalization** (including tags for case-sensitive searching), (c) unintentional **font** changes (in type, style, or size), (d) **cut-off** text (e.g., due to cell or page limitations), (e) sloppy **formatting** (lines missing or overlapping, inconsistent spacing between graphs, varied row height for no reason, etc.), or (f) inflexibility to **variations** (e.g., graph bar colors do not adhere to intended colors/meanings if an assessment has fewer proficiency levels than usual).

4.1.04 Private and Secure

Conform to best practices and legislation for data privacy and security.

4.2 KEY FEATURES

Key package/display features refer to components that can be seen within data reports. The 4.2 standards pertain to key feature design.

4.2.01 Summaries/Averages for Comparison

Include the summaries/averages that will best provide context for the types of comparisons users will want to make when they use the report (this requires understanding the report's purpose and use). E.g., a class list of 35 students' scores will likely require a "Class" row averaging each column's data.

4.2.02 Calculations Done for You

Provide calculations that prevent users from having to perform mental arithmetic when analyzing data (e.g., if displaying performance over multiple years on a vertically scaled assessment, display any appropriate, relevant growth calculations). Note calculations can also result in words rather than numbers, such as a proficiency determination.

4.2.03 Vital Data Included

Display all data required for a report to function most effectively. Do not require users to look elsewhere to acquire data a user needs (a) to **properly** use the report or (b) for the report to achieve its intended **purpose** (e.g., if users must hover or click to "drill down" to added info, that added info must not be essential to the report's primary purpose).

4.2.04 Graph as Appropriate

Include graph(s) when appropriate while adhering to graph guidelines such as: (a) use graphs **only for key info/comparisons** (e.g., use graphs to point out important occurrences – such as trends – that are easily missed in a table, but do not graph all available data), (b) select graph type based on **ease** of use and its **suitability** to the graph's purpose, (c) include **0 on the scale** of an axis (rather than narrowing its displayed range) and make the scale read from **left to right** (e.g., scales on a horizontal, such as a table's row of column headers, should begin with the lowest value in the leftmost location and end with the highest values in the rightmost location), (d) use **two-dimensional** (not 3-D) graphs, (e) place **data directly on** the graph (e.g., if a bar represents 36% of students, display "36%" above the bar), and (f) **consider # of entities** (e.g., if 78 schools would each appear as bars on a graph, rendering the graph cluttered and ineffective, default to a modified display).

4.2.05 Clear Headers

Use headers (e.g., cells that top report columns and start rows) that: (a) **provide added info** to prevent user confusion or the need to look elsewhere to understand the data's nature, (b) **distinguish/group data** (e.g., when there are varied categories of data columns, such as three columns of data for one test and three columns of data for another, use multiple header rows to clarify demarcations and reduce text repetition), (c) **avoid all caps** (only use all capital letters if absolutely necessary to help distinguish some headers from others), and (d) **repeat when printed** (column headings should repeat at the top of each subsequent page when a table continues on multiple printed pages, just as main page header info should repeat and be included with page numbers).

4.3 DESIGN

Package/display design refers to how each report looks (e.g., is arranged) on the screen and page. The 4.3 standards pertain to report display decisions.

4.3.01 Format/Components Most Appropriate for Analysis

Select the format and components most likely to encourage accurate understanding/analysis/use of the data. E.g., you might opt to use

Appendix

a table to communicate large amounts of data a report requires, but particular columns within the table can contain horizontal graph bars to highlight important data.

4.3.02 Avoid Clutter

Avoid unnecessary clutter, following guidelines such as: (a) **do not outline** bars/wedges if perimeters can survive bad printers (e.g., don't add a black line around a graph's red bar if the red is dark enough to be seen when printed on an old black and white printer), (b) **use lines sparingly** and purposefully (e.g., to distinguish sections of data rather than outlining every cell in a table), (c) include **white space** to make the report easy to understand (but not so much that it adds to excessive report pages when printed), (d) **round numbers that will not lose distinctions** (i.e., round all numbers to the whole *unless* you are dealing with small numbers for which distinctions will be lost without decimals, such as averages of performance levels ranging from just 1–5; when an extra place value is warranted, limit the decimals to one if effective), (e) **show data and eliminate other clutter** (i.e., if added data will give a report more meaning, add the data and select *other* clutter to eliminate), (f) **avoid unnecessary text/columns/rows** (e.g., if adding a table column with the calculation of performance level data comprising *% Proficient*, there is typically no need to add a column for the calculation of performance level data comprising *% Not Proficient*), and (g) **not everything experts ask for** has to be included (there are too many "recommended" additions for reports to accommodate; consider each addition against the importance of avoiding report clutter).

4.3.03 Avoid Keys/Legends

Work content into a chart's title or labels (e.g., directly within or beside graph segments such as bars or lines) to avoid a key or legend whenever possible. If legend inclusion is unavoidable, keep the order of colors/explanations in the key consistent with the order in which segments are presented in the graph.

4.3.04 Most Important Data in Prime Locations

Place the report's most important data in places likely to stand out (e.g., not lost in a table's middle columns). Treat the last column or row in a table as prime real estate, reserved for data users are most likely to need. Treat the first row and column (which come after the header row and column) as slightly less prime (but more desirable than middle columns) if additional data needs to stand out. Likewise, reserve any culminating graphics or sections for those communicating key info.

4.3.05 Juxtapose Comparisons

Offer **reports that juxtapose** multiple subgroups, other entities, years/times, or measures for easy comparison (i.e., users should not have to run separate reports to make common comparisons). Use **proximity within reports** when placing data that will need to be compared.

4.3.06 Eye Can Scan without Obstacles

Allow the user's eye to move across a report or section without encountering visual obstacles that impede common comparisons. E.g., if accompanying a table's primary data (like rows for "% of students" earning each column's performance level) with secondary data (like rows for "# of students" earning each column's performance level), give secondary data a smaller font so it is easy to ignore or compare separately when the eye scans the page.

4.3.07 Do Not Hug Lines

With few exceptions (such as widely varying figures), center or indent data horizontally within cells and center data vertically within cells rather than justifying data directly against cell borders.

4.3.08 Purposeful Color and Shading

Use color and shading purposefully and selectively (a) as an additional layer of **communication** (e.g., bars of graphed scores can be green vs. red to visually communicate if the scores rendered *Proficient* vs. *Not Proficient* status) and (b) to help **organize** a report (e.g., report section headings can be shaded to stand out and better differentiate sections).

4.3.09 Size Reflects Importance

If there are any required variations in size (e.g., font size), make sure it is appropriate for users to deem the reduced-size info as less important.

4.3.10 Not Unnecessarily Complicated or Overly Simplified

Do not make a report more complicated than it needs to be *or* more simple than it has to be. E.g., (a) use a **simple-yet-effective display** (e.g., do not simplify the data presentation to the point that it is misunderstood or less effective) and (b) use **simple language** and avoid jargon (e.g., use *# tested* rather than *n*, *average* rather than *mean*, *growth* or *improvement* rather than *gain score*, *most frequent score* rather than *mode*, etc.).

4.4 NAVIGATION

Navigation refers to the manner and ease with which users are able to use and move through the data system. The 4.4 standards pertain to navigation design.

4.4.01 Easy and Fast

Facilitate easy (e.g., logical arrangement) and fast/efficient (e.g., few clicks) use and movement within the system, remembering users' tech-familiarity varies.

4.4.02 Efficient Filters for Finding Reports

Provide filters users can select to narrow the list of available reports relevant to their needs. Provide filters that: (a) cover **major search needs** varied users are likely to have, (b) do **not cover minor search needs** (reserve this for open-ended searching), (c) utilize proper capitalization (for appearance) but do **not operate on a case-sensitive** basis (e.g., a lowercase search can lead to uppercase-tagged reports), (d) allow for **multiple tags per report** (tags are report-tied terms by which filters operate) and the ability to use multiple filters, (e) are displayed in clear, logical **categories** when users are viewing and selecting filters, and (f) are **region-specific** (to match the user's tests, etc.).

4.4.03 Consolidate Reports to Support Multiple Inquiries

Consolidate like reports into a single report (which can then be customized by the user with input controls, e.g., selecting a particular test) whenever possible.

4.4.04 Design Consistency

Remain as consistent as possible from one report to the next in terms of design as long as the design remains well-suited to the data's appropriate analysis.

4.5 INPUT CONTROLS

Input controls provide users with options (e.g., via drop-down menus) to customize how a report is generated, which allows the same report to serve multiple functions. The 4.5 standards pertain to input control design.

4.5.01 Facilitate Recommended Data Investigation Practices

Offer input controls that facilitate data investigation practices that are recommended for users. E.g., allow educators to open a single report and use its input controls to easily change the measure being viewed, rather than requiring users to select a test-specific report and then return to the report list to find and select another test-specific report in order to investigate multiple measures.

4.5.02 Required Controls Are Visible

If "hiding" some input controls (e.g., to not overwhelm users), do not hide any controls required for the report to generate.

4.5.03 Grey Out Unavailable Options and Leave Out Never-Available Options

Grey out unavailable options (e.g., any options for which there *can be* data but there is *not* data are still listed, but in a lighter/grey font). Do not display options that are never available for particular parameters (e.g., grade levels that are not taught at a particular site).

4.5.04 Categorized Control Display

Display/group input controls by category (e.g., by *Scope, Test*, and *Students*).

4.5.05 Time-Saving Options

Offer time-saving options such as: (a) easy **disaggregation** of data, (b) easy **aggregation** (e.g., among single grade level options, let users opt to select *All Tested (combined)* for *Grade Level* to generate a single report in which all grade levels' results are consolidated/summarized), (c) **run multiple reports at once** (e.g., let users opt to select *Each Tested (separate)* for *Grade Level* to generate a separate report for each grade level within a single generation so the user does not have to run each report separately), (d) data **source options** (e.g., using state/official data source files vs. the data system's local/roster-based data), and (e) **multi-select** (e.g., let users opt to select multiple options simultaneously on a single drop-down menu).

CONTENT

Just as over-the-counter products must contain effective and unexpired ingredients to function well, the contents of data systems and reports must be effective and timely. *Content* standards are organized by *Each Report* and *Report Suite*.

5.1 EACH REPORT

Each Report refers to the content of each report in a data system or report suite. The 5.1 standards pertain to report content considerations.

5.1.01 Expiration

Keep report contents current, e.g., with changing: (a) **legislation** (e.g., accountability requirements, retention criteria, terminology used, etc.), (b) **user needs** (e.g., growing term familiarity), (c) **research** developments such as those concerning users' data needs (e.g., new approaches to data use), and (d) **technology** developments (e.g., if users cannot "drill-down" or download to manipulation-friendly formats when needed, the report environment is dated).

5.1.02 Audience Appropriate

Cater design contents to the report's pre-determined audience(s) in terms of its: (a) **knowledge and skills** (e.g., terms and explanations), (b) **role** and how it will use the report (e.g., components included vs. excluded), and (c) **region** (e.g., format that best accommodates an assessment's reporting guidelines).

5.2 REPORT SUITE

Report Suite refers to the collection of reports within the data system or other reporting environment, and it concerns how the suite of reports functions as a whole. The 5.2 standards pertain to report suite considerations.

5.2.01 Expiration

Keep the report suite current, e.g., with changing: (a) **legislation** (e.g., reports addressing new forms of accountability), (b) **user needs** (e.g., sync with new edtech), (c) **research** developments such as those concerning users' data needs (e.g., the system is dated if every educator does not have access to timely data or if no reports are predictive or show progress over time), and (d) **technology** developments (e.g., the system is dated if students are not tied to unique identifiers; or if users cannot create custom reports without query-writing knowledge; or if data is not appropriately collected, stored, and protected).

5.2.02 Proactive Design Approach

Utilize a predominantly **proactive** (rather than reactive) design model for report development and maintenance where the core suite of reports is **preplanned** in a **centralized** fashion (e.g., someone with an education/data/design background should lead the project, solicit feedback, etc.).

5.2.03 Not Too Many

Do not offer so many separate reports that the report list is overwhelming and individual reports are hard to find. Instead, plan a report suite that is efficient. E.g., each report should accommodate multiple variables as options (such as an input control with multiple measures) and each report's topic should address multiple theories and questions (which can be infinite).

5.2.04 Organized to Cover Needs Matrix

Offer a suite of reports that, as a whole, meets users' key data needs (as organized within a comprehensive needs matrix) in a way that is user-friendly and unintimidating. E.g., the suite: (a) has **no gaps** (gaps occur when key analyses are not facilitated by any of a data system's reports, or when key analyses can only be accommodated when data system reports and/or features not intended for those analyses have to be used in a cumbersome way because no better alternatives exist in the data system), (b) is **topic-focused** (whereas theories and questions are infinite), and (c) is **region-specific**.

Note: Over-the-Counter Data Standards represent a synthesis of more than three hundred studies and texts from experts in the field. See Rankin publications summarizing this research. Also note standards cannot capture all design considerations that should go into each data system or report,

Appendix

so it is important to continually stay abreast of related research and recommendations. The above standards thus encompass best practices (a) most likely to have a significant impact and (b) often found missing from data systems/reports.

For Product Safety Concerns and Information please contact our EU representative GPSR@taylorandfrancis.com
Taylor & Francis Verlag GmbH, Kaufingerstraße 24, 80331 München, Germany

www.ingramcontent.com/pod-product-compliance
Lightning Source LLC
Chambersburg PA
CBHW051522230426
43668CB00012B/1699